The Making of a

purity

devotion

reconciliation

repentance

humility

servanthood

perseverance

GODLY MAN

WORKBOOK

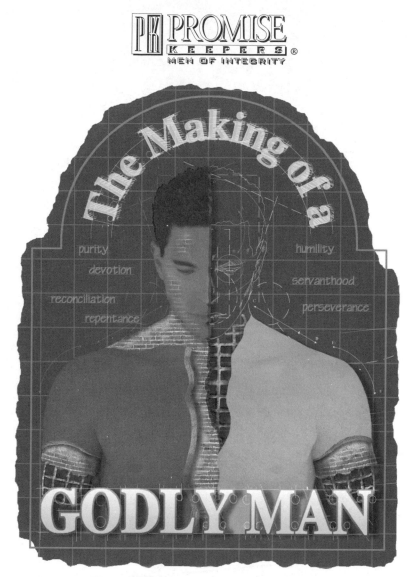

PROMISE KEEPERS ®
MEN OF INTEGRITY

The Making of a

purity
devotion
reconciliation
repentance

humility
servanthood
perseverance

GODLY MAN

WORKBOOK

A Guide to Help Men Live Out the Seven Promises

John Trent

FOCUS ON THE FAMILY ®

PUBLISHING
Colorado Springs, Colorado

to two men who have played a
crucial role in my spiritual growth:

Dr. Howard Hendricks, my professor, friend,
and mentor in family ministry

and

the Rev. Doug Barram, who first led me to Christ
and showed me, by his life and ministry,
what it takes to be a man of God

Contents

ACKNOWLEDGMENTS

In many ways, I feel as if I'm the waiter who gets all the credit for presenting a delicious meal. Actually, many hands went into this work, and a few that deserve special thanks are:

At Promise Keepers

Coach McCartney, for his vision, cutting-edge challenges, and nonstop drive to see men everywhere be men of God.

Pete Richardson, who gave birth to the idea of this workbook and first shared it with me as we stood together with 60,000 men at the Tampa Promise Keepers conference.

Dr. Rod Cooper, for his leadership and expertise in how men learn and how this workbook should be structured.

Mary Guenther, for her editing skills and for carrying the ball through all those committee meetings, gathering important feedback and additions.

At Focus on the Family

Al Janssen, my fellow "storyboarder" and good friend who kept the torch burning brightly at Focus for this project.

Larry Weeden, editor extraordinaire, who always seems to put a polish on whatever I write like 12 coats of Turtle Wax.

And to a few special friends

Doug Childress, who lifted huge weights from my shoulders here at the office; and Darryl Herringer and Ron Gardener, who have volunteered much needed help "on the road."

The Rev. Mark Wheeler, my small-group expert, for whose contributions to the exercise section of this workbook I am deeply indebted.

INTRODUCTION

I was in a hurry. I was late and needed to get to the office. I was making good time, too, but just as I was getting ready to switch lanes, someone came out of nowhere and cut me off. As I was about ready to *bless* that driver, my eye noticed a bumper sticker on his car—since I was now pretty close to his bumper.

It read, IF YOU THINK EDUCATION IS EXPENSIVE—TRY IGNORANCE.

When I settled down from my close encounter, I began to think about the truth in that message. In fact, it's biblical. Scripture says, "Without knowledge—my people perish." The Bible exhorts us to grow in Christlikeness, but we'll stay stagnant and immature if we aren't learning what it *means* to be Christlike. I've had to say on many occasions, "If I had just taken the time to understand what God says about this subject, I wouldn't have made that decision." There's only one thing worse than not knowing, and that's wishing you did.

But knowledge has two sides. *Knowing* in the Bible is not a mere intellectual exercise but also living out the truth daily. Jesus said, "He who has ears to hear—let him hear." *Knowing* without *applying* means nothing. It would be like deciding to take up jogging, reading the best books on jogging, underlining the meaningful parts of the books, buying the best jogging suit and running shoes, even giving seminars on jogging—and never once suiting up to run! Knowledge without application is actually foolishness.

Our desire at Promise Keepers is to help you truly know God. Our mission statement in the education department is Colossians 1:28, which reads, "We proclaim him, admonishing and teaching everyone with all wisdom, so that we may present everyone perfect [mature] in Christ." We want you to know Him and then use what you know to begin to experience the abundant life He has promised.

We believe you want to grow or you wouldn't have picked up this workbook. We believe you're serious about *keeping* your promises, not just *making* them. We're excited that you've made the decision to embark on a learning process to go deeper in your walk with Christ. In the following pages, we will lay out for you a clear plan and process for keeping your promises.

Now, the seven promises we espouse at Promise Keepers are not some magical formula to make you holy or guarantee success in every area of your life. Not at all. So why are there seven of them and not 10, 20, or even 30? We chose the seven we have because they crystallize for us what it means to be a man of integrity. They aren't commandments, but they are clear statements of what we believe it means, based on the Word of God, for a man to be both privately and publicly a godly man—a promise keeper.

We also want you to know something that's crucial in keeping these promises: *You can't do it in your own strength*. It's impossible. You can't have a Nike mentality—"Just do it"—and be godly. There's no cram course for character. It's a process that's dependent on the Word of God, the Spirit of God, and the people of God. In other words, keeping your promises requires both horizontal and vertical relationships. Utter dependence on God's Holy Spirit and loving accountability from your Christian brothers is what will help you to truly be a promise keeper and not just a promise maker.

You will discover, in the following chapters, the kind of context that's best for men in learning the promises; a proven strategy to help you keep your promises; and a process to sustain the promises in your life. There aren't many guarantees in life, but we guarantee this: If you will humbly submit yourself to God as you follow this plan, you *will* come to know Him better and, as a result, want to live for Him—not because you *have* to but because you *want* to.

Heavenly Father, may You bless these my brothers as they yield their lives to You in utter dependence and seek to be the men of God You have called them to be. Bless them, Father, and thank You that as You have begun a good work in them, so You will finish it.

Amen!

Rod Cooper
National Director
of Educational Ministries
Promise Keepers

Part I

The Making of a

GODLY MAN

**A LIFELONG PROCESS
FOR SPIRITUAL GROWTH**

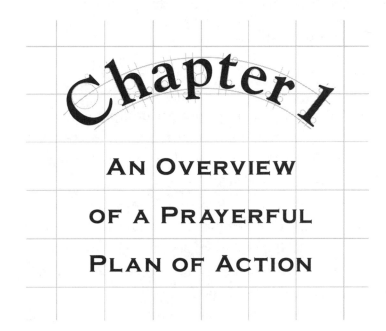

Chapter 1

AN OVERVIEW
OF A PRAYERFUL
PLAN OF ACTION

Not all grown-ups act like adults.

Take the 14 men each year (on average) who die *when soda machines fall on them*. (You guessed it: They put in their money, don't get their soda, and become so angry that they shake the machine until it tips over and crushes them!)

Or consider the two drivers recently who were speeding down a Washington, D.C., freeway, shouting and gesturing angrily at each other. Both of them failed to see an upcoming turn, lost control of their cars, crashed, and were killed!

Grown-ups act like babies regularly.

But being a "baby" has never been the goal of a committed Christian. As followers of Jesus Christ, we need to be pledged to growing in maturity, sustained by solid food, not baby food.

The apostle Paul chided the believers in Corinth for having to be fed "milk" instead of the "meat" of God's Word, the Bible. The same challenge applies to each of us. It's time to grow up to maturity in our faith, and doing so takes an active commitment to godly living.

That's why we encourage you to adopt a personal, prayed-over plan for spiritual growth. This will involve setting spiritual goals and well-thought-out challenges in specific areas that can help you "close the gap" between who you are today and who you can become in Jesus Christ.

We're not talking about creating a legalistic set of rules that shuts out the direction of the Holy Spirit. Rather, we're advocating a flexible plan of action sensitive to the leading of the Holy Spirit and dependent on His power. Such a plan involves "growing up" in seven specific aspects of godliness that are reflected in the seven promises of a Promise Keeper.

As Rod Cooper said in his Introduction, there's nothing magical or sacred about these seven promises. They're not a divine formula, nor does trying to keep them guarantee a problem-free life. However, we believe they summarize the historic core of what a sold-out life for Jesus Christ looks like.

In personalizing your own spiritual growth plan, feel free to identify an area of particular emphasis, stress a specific part of the fruit of the Spirit you want to grow in, or focus on a characteristic of an elder or deacon that you feel is important. The goal of working through the process laid out in this workbook is Christlikeness, nothing more or less.

Like unfolding a road map to trace the route we'll be taking, let's look at several key icons that represent the basic parts of this workbook. Each icon acts like a milestone marker, keeping you on track and moving you through the process we'll present.

AN OVERVIEW OF THE "CLOSING THE GAP" PROCESS

Part One: Before You Create Your Plan

Part one of this workbook contains three important introductory elements for you to read and understand:

 In the next chapter, you'll see that the first step, if we're serious about growing spiritually, is to be broken over our sin and weakness and grateful for and humbled by what Jesus has done in redeeming us.

 Even with an attitude of brokenness, however, we're not exempt in a fallen world from barriers to growth. These are discussed in chapter 3, and they factor into the plan of action you'll create as well.

 In chapter 4, you'll see that there's a powerful "context" in which men best grow and learn to surmount barriers over the long term. From the "sharpening" of one man on another in a small group, to the encouragement to turn daily commitments into lifelong habits, this context is a key to lasting change.

Part Two: Creating Your Personal Growth Plan

Creating your spiritual growth plan involves two important steps.

LOOKING BACK IN A POSITIVE WAY

Your plan begins by looking back in a positive way at some formative events in your life. More than 100 times in the Scriptures, we're encouraged to "remember ... remember ..." In Joshua 4, for example, when God had parted the Jordan River so the people of Israel could cross over on dry land, Joshua (under God's direction) had the people gather up a stone for each tribe from the river, and then he built a memorial with them so the nation would always remember the miracle God had done for them at that place.

You, too, will "step back" and remember "milestone markers" of God's goodness, as well as the personal struggles and successes that highlight your life story. You'll be encouraged to fill out several forms that provide an important historical perspective for you, your small group, and your loved ones. These forms will help you explain the "high points" and "challenge points" you've experienced. And they can help to reveal negative cycles you may need special help in overcoming.

Then it will be time to move through each of the seven promise areas and create your plan.

GAINING A CLEAR PLAN FOR LONG-TERM GROWTH

After you've looked back in a positive way, it will be time to step forward toward a deeper faith in and love for Christ. To do that, we're encouraging you to work through seven specific areas of a godly man's life.

To create your personal spiritual growth plan, simply follow the flags as you work through each of the seven promises, one per week. (You may also decide to take two weeks on each promise to do the work described below.) Take promise one, which addresses "a man and his God," for example. To develop a plan for being more sold-out in your spiritual life, you would:

Begin by looking up key verses from which the promise springs, reading a short description of the promise, and then reading a brief story of how one man lived it out. (For the purposes of this workbook, only a brief synopsis of each promise is given. If you want to go deeper into these promises, we encourage you to read *Seven Promises of a Promise Keeper* or *Go the Distance*.)

Next, you'll be challenged to make a personal evaluation of where you are today in regard to this promise. You'll also have a chance to set a goal for where you'd like to be in the future. For the purposes of this spiritual growth plan, we'll be setting a "horizon point" of three years. An evaluation form accompanies each promise.

 Now it's time for specifics. You'll find in each chapter in part two a form that encourages you to set three specific goals for that promise. These are called "action points," and they're specific actions or attitudes that you'll pray over, discuss with your small group and family, and seek to live out every day— all with the goal of becoming more like Jesus Christ.

Included with your action points form is a place to list three potential barriers to growth. These could be historical hurts or current attitudes, actions, or situations that you know have the potential to block you from putting your growth plan into action.

Now your initial plan is complete. Throughout the weeks, feel free to add to, subtract from, or update it as the Lord leads. We encourage you to discuss your initial plan with those closest to you (your spouse if you're married) and with each member of your small group. This gives them a prayer guide for encouraging you and an accountability tool for helping you keep your commitments.

Next, you're ready for the third step in the process—living it out every day!

Part Three: Going through a Series of Encouragement Cycles

To help you turn your plan into everyday actions, you'll cycle back through each promise area (one cycle of seven weeks for each promise). The order in which you do this is up to you and your small group. For example, let's say that your group talked and prayed and came up with the following order:

In this case, the group picked promise four, "A Man and His Family," as the first area to cycle through. We suggest you cycle through each promise in the following way (feeling free to tailor this process to your needs and God's leading).

CYCLING THROUGH PROMISE FOUR

We suggest that you and your small group meet once a week for seven weeks, focusing on this promise area. In your meetings, the spiritual growth plan you created would be the first springboard for discussion. Tell your small group how you've done in the past week at living out your three specific goals, as well as what you've done to face the three barriers you've listed. Ask the other men for their prayers, advice, or scriptural insights into living out your plan.

In addition, we've included specific activities in part three for you to complete and share as a group each week.

These activities are specifically designed to get you to think through this promise area more deeply, apply it more fully in your life, and provide a starting point for group discussion. For example, with promise four, there are six group activities for you to complete and share. These activities range from short self-evaluation tests, to designing a family crest, to biblical word or character studies, to challenging negative stereotypes.

In the seventh, or last, week of this and every cycle, we ask you to do something extremely important—spend your small-group time in prayer, thanksgiving, worship, and revising your plan of action as needed. You'll have worked for six weeks to improve at living out this promise. Now thank God for what He has accomplished in and through you, and ask His help to continue the good work and to face whatever barriers might have come up.

With that cycle completed (in this case, having gone through promise four), our hypothetical group is ready to work through the next promise area they've picked, and so on until they've cycled through all seven promises.

ADDITIONAL TOOLS AND AN IMPORTANT NEXT STEP

A final section of this workbook offers several additional tools, including some forms for reviewing your plan in the future and recommended resources for going deeper in the seven promises.

You've now looked at a road map of where we'll be going to help you create and live out a plan for greater Christlikeness. It's time to get in gear and begin moving in the right direction. And the first stop on our journey is to get on our knees before Almighty God.

DISCUSSION QUESTIONS

1. What most excites you about having a specific spiritual growth plan? What most concerns you? Why?

2. When Adam was confronted by God in the Garden of Eden, he first tried to hide, and then he hurled blame at his wife. When confronted with the need to change, do you tend to avoid, accept, or deny it? Why?

3. As you put together a small group of men to go through the process with you, what's your greatest challenge? What's the thing to which you most look forward?

4. On a scale from 1 (not at all) to 10 (totally), how committed are you to growing in Christlikeness? Be honest with your answer.

5. What could move that number closer to 10?

Chapter 2

BROKENNESS:

THE FIRST STEP

TOWARD

CHRISTLIKENESS

Imagine you're standing on the track in an Olympic stadium. More than 100,000 people are crammed into the stands, tense with excitement. While you try valiantly to shove it out of your mind, you also know more than *500 million* households across the world are looking on via television.

It's the last few moments before your race, and as you walk around, you shake yourself in a vain attempt to relax, looking down at your gold shoes and new track uniform with the distinctive "swoosh."

Suddenly, an official blows a whistle, signaling that it's time for all contestants to get ready to race.

Quietly, you walk to the starting line. You shake your arms and take deep breaths to try to relax.

"Set!" comes the command, and with the other contestants, you raise your eyes to the horizon, your adrenaline soaring. It seems as if the world collectively holds its breath on this warm summer's morning, waiting for the sound of the starter's gun.

An eerie, enduring silence . . . and then, finally . . .

Bang!

There it is!

Your long-distance race is on, detonating a wild explosion of noise, emotion, and cheers from the assembled crowd. Cameras are clicking, and the racers bolt for position at the front of the pack.

Only you're not with them.

In fact, you still haven't left the starting line.

Can you imagine the confusion amidst the cameras and commentators if, instead of shooting forward with all your own effort and energy at the sound of the starter's pistol, your first step was to slump to your knees? Not in confusion, injury, or admission of defeat, but in wisdom, brokenness, and victory.

That isn't how Olympic marathons are won, but it is a word picture of the starting point for this *Making of a Godly Man Workbook*. The book you hold is not an exercise in self-effort or a plan designed to play well to a worldly crowd—or even a Christian crowd that doesn't have its priorities straight. It's not centered in chasing fading glory or winning you wealth or fame. Actually, it's a challenge to live a sold-out life of faith before Almighty God, the starting place for long-term spiritual growth and an abundant life.

BROKENNESS: THE STARTING POINT
FOR GOD TO CHANGE YOUR LIFE

 How willing are you to be "broken" before the Lord? Such a willingness is the starting point for spiritual growth. It's not an option but a requirement. God's Word tells us that He "resists the proud" but gives His grace, power, love, and peace to those with pliable, teachable, humble hearts.

In the chapters that follow, you'll find a positive, prayerful plan of action to help you become more like Jesus Christ. But it's simply not a plan for proud people.

Proud people don't think they need to be taught; they won't admit they have areas of weakness in which they need to grow, and they won't acknowledge their need for others.

Proud people may *feel* a deep need for God to make dramatic changes in their lives, but only if He'll do so on their terms.

Proud people could be someone like you or me . . . or a man named Naaman.

In 2 Kings 5, we find that Naaman was a mighty warrior in a nation known for military prowess. He had success, chevrons, and a special place in his king's heart. He had won often and decisively in one-on-one combat, yet he was losing a greater battle and his life to a horrible, incurable disease.

Fortunately, this mighty warrior had captured more than just prisoners and loot from one of his recent forays inside the nation of Israel. His men had brought back a young girl to be a household servant—a child who was convinced she knew someone who could help her new master.

When we look in on in 2 Kings, we see something almost comical. Naaman knew he had a terrible problem and couldn't cure himself, yet he still wasn't willing to admit he was powerless! He did humble himself slightly in listening to a servant girl and seeking the aid of a foreign prophet. But even then he went proudly, wearing his finest dress uniform and taking along loads of treasure and an armed contingent as menacing as any Airborne Ranger unit.

He was desperate, so he rode to get help—but only on his own terms! He didn't go in brokenness or humility to the man of God the girl had described. In fact, *he didn't go to see Elisha at all!* He went to someone he thought could be of better help and certainly had a better image—the king of Israel. However, when he showed up on the king's doorstep, that man of little faith panicked and tore his robe, crying, "Who can help you except God alone?"

That's when Elisha, God's servant, got into the act by scolding the king and sending one of his servants to give Naaman an almost nonsensical ultimatum: "Wash in the river Jordan seven times, and you will be clean."

You can imagine the inner battle fought by Naaman after that. He had already gone to a small desert kingdom to seek a cure. Then, instead of getting royal treatment, he was handed off to the *servant* of some religious man with no standing or station. And now, he was asked to do something that wasn't just humbling, it was *humiliating!*

Strip naked—in a culture of extreme modesty—and bathe in a muddy river that couldn't hold a candle to any of a dozen mighty streams in his homeland? Never would he become that compliant; never would he humble himself that much. He had his pride. He would not be broken! Not on his life!

Yet his life depended on his willingness to be broken, to bow in recognition that he couldn't do anything to save himself. Obeying God's word, spoken through His prophet, was his only hope.

Naaman wanted to change, but he wanted to do so by staying in control and maintaining his image. So he stomped off. But thankfully, in stepped a special friend. Naaman had that rare type of friend who is willing to confront even a powerful, prideful man and challenge him with the truth—and a test.

His friend explained that if Elisha had asked Naaman to do something difficult—even next to impossible—he'd have done it in a heartbeat. That's good insight. Completing some difficult task through self-effort would have appealed to Naaman's proud and self-reliant male spirit. But Elisha, speaking on behalf of Almighty God, didn't give Naaman that option.

God isn't interested in proud men who hold tightly to their symbols of status or wealth. He's searching for hearts that are broken, obedient, pliable, and willing to step out in faith—and into a river if He tells them to.

Wisely, that's just what Naaman did. Finally broken, he humbled himself totally and stepped naked into the water seven times. Dramatically, miraculously, he stepped out with baby-smooth skin. Flesh that had carried a graphic picture of sin and death was now washed clean by obeying God's word.

Get the picture?

Perhaps you bent your pride enough to go to a Promise Keepers stadium event or wake-up call. Maybe you've been challenged by friends, family, or circumstance to get serious about your faith. Your need for change might be even more dramatic than was Naaman's. Perhaps you're facing a medical or personal ultimatum, or you just know deep inside that if things don't change in your life, you'll lose everything.

Don't think you can become more of a man of God by seeking to change *while still holding on to your power and prestige*. He *alone* is the King of kings. He tolerates no self-inflated monarchs. If you're serious about changing your life, it begins by being a broken servant before Him.

Some might say, "But I'm not sure what you mean by brokenness." To help you understand better, here are two further aspects of brokenness to consider:

BREAKING THROUGH THE "SELF-EFFORT" CEILING

Why can't you do it on your own? What about rugged individualism? Take a look at the diagram below. It illustrates something that affects every man.

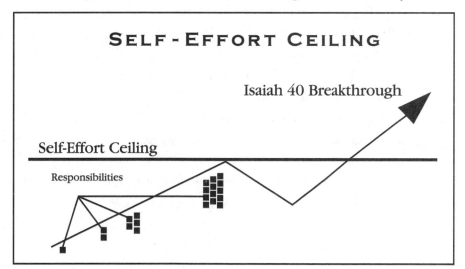

In today's culture, men are told from their earliest days on the playground, to the athletic fields of their youth, to the working world they labor in daily, that rugged individualism is what counts. We don't need others. We just need to suck it up, say it doesn't hurt, and shy away from admitting we're vulnerable, weak, or confused. And above all, we have to keep up the image of being on top of things, even if everything's falling apart. In short, never admit you're broken.

It's a biblical fact that every man reading this book who is living by self-effort will one day hit a "ceiling of self-effort." Let me explain.

No matter how high we move up the ladder of success, every step brings with it added responsibility and emotional and relational demands. Often, when we're in our twenties and thirties and on the up-slope, we don't think there'll ever be a limit to what we can accomplish with self-effort—but there always is.

All of us hit a ceiling when family, church, work, and/or personal responsibilities become so great that we seem to "top out" and we can't handle any more or go any further. Once we hit this "ceiling of self-effort," we have no room or time for future growth—but plenty of opportunity to burn out, grow stale in our faith and commitment, and slide backward.

The church in Ephesus (see Ephesians 2) hit this ceiling. The people there had done many things well. "I know your deeds," said the resurrected Lord Jesus, "your hard work and your perseverance. I know that you . . . have tested those who claim to be apostles but are not. . . . Yet I hold this against you: You have forsaken your first love" (Revelation 2:2, 4).

They had worked and worked, yet all their positive religious self-effort did was give them an "image" of righteousness without the peace and fulfillment that come from a right heart attitude.

Can you see how mere activity—even if it's going to church or following through on the growth program presented in this workbook—can never substitute for intimacy with God? You can't work your way closer to God's heart through self-effort any more than Naaman could work his own cure for leprosy.

The prophet Isaiah put it this way: "Even youths grow tired and weary, and young men stumble and fall" (Isaiah 40:30). That's proof positive that even the most in-shape or successful will one day wear out and fail if they try to do it all on their own.

Thank God, however, there is an antidote to striving on our own and failing! What breaks through this self-effort ceiling is rest and trust, not more activity. In Isaiah's words, "But those who hope in the LORD will renew their strength. They will soar on wings like eagles; they will run and not grow weary, they will walk and not be faint" (Isaiah 40:31).

That's how you break through the ceiling of self-effort—by being broken enough to trust and "wait" when you want to work and achieve through your own strength. When you humble yourself and seek His power, you find a God who is "the LORD ..., the Creator of the ends of the earth. He will not grow tired or weary, and his understanding no one can fathom. He gives strength to the weary and increases the power of the weak" (Isaiah 40: 28-29).

In this workbook, we're asking you to create a prayerful "plan of action" to help you become more like Jesus Christ. But remember, it's not a call to greater self-effort but to greater trust in God. It will mean nothing if it ends up as a checklist of do's and don'ts instead of a tool for greater faith and growing closer to Him.

Have you hit the "ceiling of self-effort"? You can get through it only by being broken and allowing God's strength and counsel to help you move toward His best.

BROKENNESS ISN'T BARGAINING

The second aspect of brokenness we need to consider is that it's *not* the same as bargaining with God. Many men become convicted of their need to change and try bargaining instead. "Lord," they may say, "You're right. I can't do it on my own. I've failed miserably. My family knows it. I know it. I ask for Your strength and help to live a life that pleases You every day."

Up to that point, the prayer and heart desire are great. But then comes the bargain: "And Lord, since I'm going to change so much, I'm sure you'll change my wife ... my child ... my work situation ... my financial status ..."

In Matthew 20:1-16, we see an example of the danger of trying to bargain with God instead of loving and serving Him with open hands. It's found in the parable of the "workers." It's the story of a landowner who hired workers throughout the day to work in his vineyard.

Dr. Howard Hendricks, my professor, friend, and mentor in family ministry, taught me the importance of looking at the context that precedes a parable. In this case, in Matthew 19, the rich young ruler had just come before the Lord, seeking to justify himself. Yet he had walked away crestfallen because he refused to be broken. The Lord saw that the love of money was holding him back from life in Christ, so He called on him to give it away and follow Him.

Peter watched the whole exchange and, in confusion, asked Jesus, "What do we get out of following You and leaving everything?"

Jesus assured him that the disciples' sold-out commitment would be greatly rewarded—but then He warned Peter not to bargain. And He did so by telling the parable of the land owner and the workmen.

Looking at the story, there were, in fact, five groups of workers. They were hired by a wealthy man looking for help in his fields. That was a common practice during Jesus' day, with employers and potential workers meeting at the city gate, the center of trade and commerce.

"Early in the morning," the men in the first group struck a bargain with the land owner for one denarius for one day's work—a standard wage. Then they headed out to the fields at 6:00 A.M. for a full day's work.

"About the third hour" (9:00 A.M. in biblical times), and again at the "sixth hour" (noon), the land owner needed more workers. So he went out and found additional helpers. He hired still more at the "ninth hour" (3:00 P.M.) and the "eleventh hour" (5:00 P.M.). Please notice! *All these men in the later groups were hired without a bargain being struck.* They were simply told to go and work hard, and each man would be paid a fair wage.

The work day for a Hebrew laborer ended at 6:00 P.M., and following custom, all the workers went to the land owner at that time to receive their wages. Beginning with the men who had worked only one hour, the land owner paid each a denarius—the amount of a full day's work!

Can you imagine what each man felt, beginning with those hired last? Those hired during the eleventh hour certainly went away praising the land owner's generosity, and they probably rushed home to tell their families, "A full day's pay for only one hour of work! What a boss! Let's have steak tonight!"

So, too, the men who worked only three hours would say, "What a generous land owner I worked for today! Look what he paid me! Let's have barbecued chicken tonight!" Those who worked half a day for full pay would say, "What a guy! Let's grill hamburgers!" Even those who worked three-fourths of a day would probably say, "My boss treated me so well! Let's go to Taco Bell!"

Every single man who worked that day walked away grateful and full of praise for the land owner—*except those in the first group.* They were angry, not grateful; indignant, not full of praise. Why? Because they had *bargained* for their reward. They didn't leave it up to a gracious land owner.

This parable, a picture of how God treats His people, offers several lessons for the man who would seek to strike a bargain with God as he goes through this *Making of a Godly Man Workbook.* Let me highlight two of them.

First, length of service has *nothing* to do with the reward God gives. Perhaps you've come to Christ late in life or are coming back to Him after long years of wandering. You should know that Almighty God isn't concerned with how long you've worked for Him or how much time He's got left to use you. He just wants willing servants, not men who are "standing around." There are fields ripe for spiritual harvest, and He wants you—at any age or hour—serving Him.

Second, God is generous. Who else would pay someone a whole day's pay for less than a day's labor? *And that's the point.* God is good and gracious. As you go through this process of creating and then living out a prayerful plan of action, do it solely to please Him. Don't say, "Lord, I'm giving up extra sleep to get up and meet with the men in my small group. I'm going to be reading Your Word and seeking to serve You more than ever. So Lord, because I'm doing all this, please give me the job change I need . . ."

Don't bargain with a gracious God. Simply seek to love Him more and serve Him better, and let Him bring the rewards.

You're about to launch into a personal, prayerful growth plan that I trust will help you become more like Christ than ever before. But remember that as you begin, your first step should be to fall on your knees—broken and not bargaining for Him to do something for you, but committed more than ever to living for Him each day.

Don't kid yourself, however. If being broken before God and getting more serious about your relationship with Him sounds good to you, it sounds *terrible* to the hater of your soul, Satan. We're in a spiritual battle, Scripture tells us, at war with forces that want to put up barriers, or encourage you to build your own, to your spiritual growth.

Therefore, take a long look at the next chapter. It outlines several specific barriers common to many men and encourages you not to let them become roadblocks to your life of faith.

DISCUSSION QUESTIONS

1. Early in this chapter, we saw a list of common attributes of a proud person. Since mankind's fall into sin, we've all struggled with pride to some degree. As you read the statements below, which reflection of pride do you struggle with the most in your daily life? Share your answer with your group.

Proud people don't need to be taught. (Are you teachable or defensive?)

They aren't willing to admit they have areas of weakness. (Is it hard for you to admit your faults or failings?)

They won't acknowledge their need for others, nor will they look honestly at how their behavior is affecting others. (Do you tend to "go it alone," without asking for others' help or feedback?)

Proud people may *feel* a deep need for God to make a dramatic change in their lives, but only if those changes are made on their terms. (Do you find you get convicted by a sermon or something in Scripture, but you put off changing until you're "ready" or things are "just right"?)

2. Naaman the leper in 2 Kings 5, and even Peter and the disciples in the New Testament, struggled with pride because they were protecting their image. What good can come from caring about how others see us? When does that concern become a bad thing?

3. What steps can we take to move toward genuine brokenness before God?

Chapter 3

BARRIERS TO
LASTING CHANGE

Sometimes—*like it or not*—life changes in a flash.

That was literally true for a man named David Bloom, who told his story to a hushed audience at a news conference in San Francisco's City Hospital. It seems that Mr. Bloom's son had a pet rat named Vermin. An unusually active rat, Vermin took every opportunity to make a break for freedom when his cage door was accidentally left open. Unfortunately, this most recent time, he ran out of the bedroom, into the kitchen, and through an open door into the garage.

"As usual, he was looking for a place to hide," Mr. Bloom explained.

Vermin saw what looked like the perfect hiding place—an inviting, dark tunnel—and ran up the exhaust pipe of Mr. Bloom's motorcycle.

"I tried dangling some food on a string to draw him out, but he wouldn't come," he said.

"So I struck a match, thinking the light would attract him."

When Mr. Bloom lit the match, the flame instantly ignited a pocket of trapped gasoline, shooting a flame out the tailpipe that burned off his mustache and gave him second-degree burns. Tragically, the flame *also* ignited the rat's fur and whiskers, which in turn ignited a pocket of gas farther up the tailpipe.

That caused an explosion that blew the rat out of the tailpipe like a cannonball, striking Mr. Bloom in the face and breaking his nose! After he was released from the hospital, his son was grounded for six weeks.

That's a type of change that takes place in an instant, without advance planning or intentional action on our part. (Obviously, you don't plan to turn a rat into a flaming missile!) But the type of change we're calling men to make in this book doesn't happen by lighting a match or snapping our fingers. No man will ever go to bed a baby Christian and wake up the next morning a person of mature faith.

Our *conversion* may be as dramatic as an explosion. However, spiritual growth is more than just a single exciting moment.

Saul's life changed in a split second when he was blinded by Christ's light, yet he spent years learning about and serving Him. In the same way, Peter was overwhelmed when He saw Jesus "transfigured" before him on a mountaintop. Like any of us who would gain a glimpse of heaven's glory here on earth, Peter wanted to capture the moment forever—even to build a house and move in on the mountaintop! Yet God told him to go back down the hill and into daily life.

Perhaps you've had a "mountaintop" experience at a Promise Keepers event. It's hard to leave a stadium full of men who were strangers when you walked in and brothers when you walked out. But spiritual growth isn't about a single experience or emotion. It's about making daily decisions—over weeks, months, and years—to walk worthy of our high calling in Jesus Christ.

If you've decided to make a wholehearted stand for Christ, we're behind you 100 percent. We feel strongly that the spiritual growth plan presented in this book will help you and your small group become more like Jesus Christ. But keep in mind that the spiritual armor you're called to put on in Ephesians 6 is not so you can march in a parade. You're told to put on defensive armor and pick up the sword of truth because you're in a spiritual battle.

OUR INCREDIBLE RESISTANCE TO MAKING CHANGES

If you think deciding to go on a diet is a challenge, just wait until you decide to become a sold-out servant of the living Lord Jesus! That's the last thing Satan, or even your "old self," wants you to do (see Ephesians 4:17-32).

Let's not kid ourselves. Change is hard. Even faced with overwhelming pressure to change from a spouse, employer, or Christian friend, making deep, lasting changes in our spiritual and personal lives can take significant work and be steadfastly avoided. Several common barriers often arise when we try to make positive changes. You may not face every barrier we'll examine, but you can count on opposition. There's too much at stake for Satan to let you grow uncontested, and being forewarned about these common barriers can help you anticipate and overcome them. Specifically, we'll look at three fears and then three additional barriers to growing in Christ.

In the book of Proverbs, we're told that a wise king decides, while the enemy is yet far off, whether he should go to war. We pray that you'll count the cost and be prepared to "go the distance," to complete this workbook and commit to long-term growth. Toward that end, let's look at a man who lct fear keep him from needed change.

FELIX, THE FEARFUL GOVERNOR

Have you ever been convicted of your need to change, only to have that rock-solid conviction turn to lukewarm action? What stood in your way? If you're like a man named Felix, it's the small word *fear* that has the potential to stop you dead in your tracks.

Felix was a Roman governor with a beautiful wife named Drusilla. By every account, Felix was a godless pagan. He was even reported to have murdered his own brother so he could marry the brother's wife—*Drusilla!* Yet Drusilla was a Jewess and apparently talked much about spiritual matters with Felix. Thus, when the apostle Paul landed in Felix's jail, this powerful ruler was curious and even eager to talk with him.

Here's how the Scriptures summarize one of their discussions:

> He sent for Paul and listened to him as he spoke about faith in Christ Jesus. As Paul discoursed on righteousness, self-control and the judgment to come, Felix was afraid and said, "That's enough for now! . . . When I find it convenient, I will send for you." (Acts 24:24-25)

Paul stood in chains and talked about "righteousness, self-control and the judgment to come." Isn't it amazing that a Roman governor, with the power of a Roman legion at his fingertips, became afraid? Why did he? A closer look at the words Paul used will give us a clue.

The first punch to Felix's pagan lifestyle came when Paul talked about *righteousness*. In the Scriptures, this word carries with it the idea of "staying between the lines." Think of driving in a storm, and suddenly your visibility turns to zero and you can't see the white lines in front of you. Particularly if you're in the fast lane, not being able to keep your car between the lines can be deadly. The same principle is true in our daily lives as well.

Wandering outside the lines of God's Word, you're a wreck waiting to happen. Paul challenged Felix to quit his reckless and wandering lifestyle and lead a godly life "between the lines" of God's will and Word.

Then Paul threw a hard left hook when he talked about *self-control*. This word has behind it the picture of "pulling on the reins" of a horse. When we keep a close rein on our actions, attitudes, and appetites, we have self-control. When we're undisciplined and let our desires, appetites, or anger run free (so free they "cross the line" of righteousness), we're not showing self-control. This was a second hard blow to Felix's godless lifestyle and set him up for the knockout punch.

Finally, Paul talked about *the judgment to come*. There's no way to sugarcoat the terrible end of those who die apart from knowing Jesus Christ. It's not just "fire and brimstone." Hell is also the only place in the universe, as C. S. Lewis said, where you're "safe" from God's love.

I'm convinced that Paul described not just the judgment of a life apart from Christ, but also the way to turn away God's wrath. That's the gospel, and Felix needed to trust Jesus Christ as his Lord and Savior.

As believers in Christ, we don't face eternal separation from His light and love. But that doesn't mean we're free to live a sinful life just because we're forgiven. As Paul wrote, "Shall we go on sinning so that grace may increase? By no means!" (Romans 6:1-2). Additionally, conviction can come to the Christian for not sharing the gospel with a relative or loved one who does face that judgment.

Righteousness, self-control and the judgment to come

Take a moment now to write down (and discuss with your small group) a specific attitude or instance where you became convicted in one (or more) of these areas:

Righteousness (keeping your life between the lines)

_____

_____

_____

Self-control (pulling on the reins)

_____

_____

_____

The judgment to come (fear of judgment for you or a loved one)

_____

_____

_____

Without a doubt, Paul's words hit Felix right between the eyes. Hearing of his need for righteousness, self-control, and a Savior, we're told, *"Felix was afraid."*

Felix was convicted of his need to change, but fear got in the way. And like many of us, when he became afraid, he opted for *procrastination,* not action.

"Felix was afraid and said, 'That's enough for now!'"

Three kinds of fear in particular can create barriers to needed change. Take a look at these, and evaluate how they've affected your own life.

FEAR OF SUCCESS OR FAILURE

With success come heightened expectations that can be hard to live up to, especially over the long haul. Or perhaps deep down you're fearful that if you really get serious about your faith, those at work or in your extended family will ridicule you or even use it to harm you. Maybe, on the other hand, you fear failure, and as a result, you've never even tried to put together a growth plan. After all (you think), you'll just mess it up as you have other things in the past.

Do you find yourself reluctant to make changes because of fear of failure or fear that the more you do, the more will be expected of you? Write out your response below, along with your reasons:

_____

_____

_____

_____

FEAR OF INTIMACY

Still others of us may find a barrier in the fact that becoming more like Christ means we have to become more intimate with others. The closer we are to God and our fellow man, the less physical and emotional "hiding space" we'll have. No more keeping others at arm's length. No more staying isolated because we pride ourselves on our "independence."

Does your life show a pattern of fearing close relationships? Do you sense your need for them, but for whatever reason, you prefer distance to closeness with God or others? Write your response below:

_____

_____

_____

_____

FEAR OF BEING CONTROLLED

Fear of success, failure, or intimacy can take away our desire (or even our plans) to change. But for Felix, perhaps the greatest fear was of having to give up all power and pretext and humbly accept Jesus as his Lord and Savior. That was the only antidote to the sin and ultimate separation from God that he faced, but he was still afraid to make such a total commitment of his life.

Can you relate to this fear of giving control of your life to Jesus Christ? Record your response and your reasons below:

_____

_____

_____

_____

A key part of the spiritual growth plan in this book will be to identify potential barriers you may face. You've now seen three fear-based barriers that can push you into procrastination and hold you back from experiencing God's best. Don't discount their ability to keep you stuck with only a superficial faith. And don't end up like Felix, who finally did call for Paul to come back—but not to repent or make needed changes: "At the same time he was hoping that Paul would offer him a bribe, so he sent for him frequently and talked with him. When two years had passed, Felix was succeeded by Porcius Festus, but because Felix wanted to grant a favor to the Jews, he left Paul in prison" (Acts 24:26-27).

Felix wanted to have his ears tickled and perhaps even "cash in" on this man of God, but he was never willing to become like him. To do that, he would have had to truly face his fears and deal with "righteousness, self-control and the judgment to come."

How about you? Are you facing one of these fear-based barriers to going all out for Jesus Christ?

THREE ADDITIONAL BARRIERS

We Forget Our True Identity

Satan wants us to define ourselves by our weaknesses, to develop a failure focus rather than a faith focus. When we look at our identity, it's critical that we start at the cross. If we've confessed our sins and asked Jesus to be our Savior, we've been born again. Because of His completed work on the cross, we have many strengths. Yet when we're in the midst of battle or we've fallen, we aren't likely to be aware of them or of who the Bible says we are in Jesus. But that's exactly what we must train ourselves to do. What are some of those strengths? How about the following for a start? (Look these up on your own or in your small group.)

- We've been justified and have peace with God (see Romans 5:1).
- We're free from condemnation (see Romans 8:1-4).
- We're the righteousness of God in Christ (see 2 Corinthians 5:21) and are partakers of the divine nature (see 2 Peter 1:4).
- We've received the Spirit of God into our lives (see 1 Corinthians 2:12).
- We've been baptized into the Body of Christ (see 1 Corinthians 12:13).
- We've been given the mind of Christ (see 1 Corinthians 2:16).
- We have direct access to God through Christ (see Ephesians 3:12).

God knows we're weak and will make mistakes—that we aren't perfect. But don't let the barrier of past failure or even present mistakes convince you it's not worth trying to grow. Don't forget who *you* are in Jesus Christ.

We Set Unrealistic Goals

It doesn't matter what color we are, how much money we have, or how many degrees we've earned; we all tend to set unrealistic goals. There's something masculine about doing the extreme, the outrageous, the impossible. If it's risky, if no one has ever done it before (and lived to tell about it), it's something for a "real man" to try. If it's small, it must be insignificant. If it's simple, it must be simplistic. In either case, it's not for a real man.

The summer Olympics in 1992 provided a great example of this myth. In anticipation of the Games, Reebok invested more than $15 million in ads asking whether Dan O'Brien or Dave Johnson was the world's greatest decathlete. They were both considered a slam dunk to make the U. S. Olympic team and compete in Barcelona.

Everything went great until it came to the pole vault event at the U. S. Olympic Trials. The bar started at 14 feet, 5 ¼ inches. O'Brien had cleared this height and more hundreds of times. He could do it in his sleep. So rather than play it safe and pick up some points by making a few easy vaults, he decided to pass at several lower heights before opening at 15 feet, 9 inches.

The athletic world was shocked when he failed on all three attempts to clear the bar. He went under it on his first and third attempts and knocked it off the supports while coming down on the second. If he had cleared even the lowest of the lower vaults—just 14 feet, 5 ¼ inches—he would have earned enough points to finish second in the Trials and make the Olympic team. But that was too easy. And because of his decision, he spent the 1992 Olympics in the broadcasting booth rather than on the field.

God wants us to dream great dreams and attempt great things. But He knows we need to do them *one step at a time*. When Israel took the Promised Land, they did it one city at a time. To climb one of the beautiful mountains of Colorado requires a commitment to taking one step at a time. And maturity in the Christian life comes one day, one step, one victory at a time.

The spiritual growth plan you'll develop as a part of this book is designed to give you a realistic set of goals, to identify specific barriers you may face, and to give you a platform for supportive, loving accountability—small, daily steps toward Christlikeness, not out-of-reach, unrealistic goals.

We Keep "Eclairs" in Our Refrigerator

Jay Carty, a former pro basketball player who's now an outstanding Christian speaker, has a wonderful way of picturing a barrier many men face. It's called "keeping eclairs in your refrigerator."

Let's say you decide to go on a diet. You tell your wife you're committed to this diet. You even join a small support group of other dieters who are going to hold you accountable. But you do one last thing before starting your diet.

On your way home from work, you stop by your favorite bakery and buy a dozen chocolate-covered, Boston-cream-filled eclairs. Then, when you get home, you put them in your refrigerator.

That's how you start your diet . . . with a dozen eclairs in your refrigerator. See the problem? You haven't started a diet at all. You're just saying you are and then leaving at arm's reach a convenient way to fail.

That brings me to an important question as you begin this spiritual growth process. Do you have "eclairs in your refrigerator"? Are there specific areas of sin, or "secret sins," that you haven't confessed and you don't intend to surrender to Christ? For example, are you "committed" to keeping your eyes pure, yet you have a hidden stash of pornographic magazines or videos you haven't thrown out?

You may not think an eclair can become a barrier, but it can. A double-minded man is someone who would start a spiritual growth plan and yet try to keep some area of sin intact. Take time right now to repent, confess, and toss out any eclairs that may hold you back. Below is a way for you to do that. If you mean it, pray this prayer:

> Lord, I know I'm weak. I do want to change and live sold out for You. But Lord, it's tempting to keep one foot back in the world while I try to step forward with You. I know I can't be a double-minded man and expect to have You honor and bless my prayers and efforts. So I confess to You my sin and my need to clear out the refrigerator of any eclairs I'm still keeping there. For me, those eclairs represent: _____

> Lord, I want to be a clean vessel, fit for Your use. Thank You for Your love, Your forgiveness, and Your new mercies every morning. Thank You, too, that I have some friends to help hold me accountable, and a family and loved ones who will only grow more in love with You as I do.
>
> In the name of the almighty God, the Rock of Ages, our Lord Jesus Christ, I pray.
>
> _____
> (Your name)
>
> _____
> (Date I cleaned out my refrigerator)

Please, don't go any further until you can honestly sign and date the prayer above. And don't forget that as you go through the rest of the workbook, you may well be challenged by one or more of the barriers described above.

DISCUSSION QUESTIONS

1. Out of all the barriers listed above, which one do you feel is most likely to block your path toward significant growth? Why is that so, and what's one way you can protect against it?

2. Describe a time in the past when you set a goal or even started a spiritual-growth program and failed to achieve the growth you desired. What did you learn from that experience that can help you move forward today?

3. What's one eclair that keeps showing up in your refrigerator? Talk about this with your group (and your spouse if you're married). What suggestions do they have that can help you appropriate more of God's strength in this area?

4. Is there a barrier not covered in this chapter that you want special prayer to overcome? If so, please share it with your spouse and small group.

Chapter 4

A CONTEXT FOR BREAKING THROUGH BARRIERS

Take a healthy organism and inject it with cancer-causing agents and you've soon got a body wracked with a wasting and debilitating disease. You've also got a picture of what has happened in many churches' and men's lives over the past 50 years. But this "cancer" isn't the physical variety. *Rather, like a slow but steadily growing cancer in the church and in their spiritual lives, men have quit taking seriously a relationship with Jesus Christ.*

In this chapter, we'll look briefly at what happened in our culture that drew so many men away from claiming Christ. Then we'll look closely at a "context" for engaging men today that is dramatically "reversing that curse." This same positive context for growth will help you and your small group stay together, focused on living out your spiritual growth plan and dealing with the barriers to a life of faith that we saw in the last chapter.

AN UNHEALTHY HISTORY OF MEN OF FAITH
IN OUR COUNTRY

In the United States and other countries, the horrors and devastation of World War II raised major questions in many men's minds about God's sovereignty, and in some cases even about His existence. One of the most popular songs during the 1940s, for example, was Cab Calloway's "It Ain't Necessarily So." In pointed words, it made fun of several well-known Bible stories and questioned the truthfulness of Scripture.

Bertrand Russell, a noted scholar, has said, "Let me write the songs for a nation and I don't care who writes the laws." Many men in the World War II era, faced with questions of meaning and purpose, stuffed their war memories and emotions deep inside and threw themselves into the explosion of business growth and materialism during the 1950s. Disconnected from their feelings and often from their families, they got one unwanted result: the radical rebellion of their children in the 1960s.

Now questions about everything that had to do with the "establishment"— including the church—weren't whispered but shouted. Songs like John Lennon's "Imagine," which encouraged people to imagine there were no churches, climbed the charts. "God Is Dead!" headlines filled the magazine racks, and men began not just drifting but leaving "the faith of their fathers" in droves.

Amid the heartaches of Vietnam and Watergate, and with compulsory prayer now legally outlawed in our schools, the United States was *officially* left without a moral compass. The "free love" culture was now free to shout down any absolutes and encourage people to "love the one you're with," not stand on outdated traditions like marriage or biblical fidelity.

By the 1970s, our cultural conscience was so seared with sex, drugs, and acid rock that it's no wonder we saw an explosion of the *I'm getting mine!* "rights" movements. With no need to honor God or serve others, the United States (and Western culture generally) splintered into special interest groups, each claiming its view of life was right.

By the 1980s, the loss of our moral compass and the promotion of selfishness had led to an incredible increase in crime, astronomical rises in sexually transmitted diseases, a decay in education, and a general lack of meaning and purpose. Yet with all these growing problems, our universities and media continued to call Christianity "irrelevant." To be a Christian was an insupportable matter of "faith" (spoken in a dismissive way). Science, psychologists, and self were the celebrated gods. Being an outspoken Christian man was looked on with social suspicion at best, or as backward and intolerant at worst. In part as a result of that, statistics showed that by 1980, the average church was composed of 59 percent women and only 41 percent men.

On screen and in print, our culture demeaned and defamed those who claimed the name of Christ.

Incredible.

In 50 short years, a nation that was founded by men of faith and had maintained the Bible as the central standard of right and wrong for centuries came to look at believers as irrelevant relics—likc manual typewriters in an age of computers. "Jesus Christ didn't die for me," rails an angry media magnate whose outspoken agnosticism epitomizes a world "always learning but never able to acknowledge the truth" (2 Timothy 3:7).

Men, let me just say it: *We live in a post-Christian culture.*

There are still churches on many street corners, and more revival is going on today than in some past decades. But we who claim the name of Christ no longer do so in a culture that believes in or actively supports our faith.

If you're serious about building a life and family on Jesus Christ, you can't count on our Western culture to support you. That's not to say that God can't do a miraculous work and lead entire nations to repent, like what Jonah witnessed in Nineveh. But revival and spiritual growth aren't going to happen from the top down. If a country turns to God, it will be because of individual men and women committed to growing, not because of political or social institutions.

But though it may sound contradictory, individual growth doesn't take place best in isolation. The strongest context for growth is the same one that has called more than 2 million men to Promise Keepers conferences in its first six years.

It's a masculine context that can help you "go the distance" with your spiritual growth plan and change your life, your family, and your nation as a result.

A "PERSONAL CULTURE" OF SPIRITUAL GROWTH

In spite of the bad news of where our culture is today, don't despair! God isn't dead, and neither are His men. For a long time, it almost seemed as if Christian men were in hiding or were somehow afraid to step forward in their faith. Perhaps they were just waiting to be called out.

Back in the Old Testament, when Elisha was hounded by Arab and Jezebel and felt abandoned and all alone, he was shocked to discover there were still thousands of men "whose knees have not bowed down to Baal" in Israel (1 Kings 19:18). I'm convinced that many men were shocked to discover the same thing on a summer's day in Boulder, Colorado, in 1991.

At the first official Promise Keepers event, people were amazed that more than four thousand men showed up at a basketball arena at the University of Colorado. But when those men stepped into the arena that night—and looked around at all those other men—something miraculous happened.

It was so miraculous that 24,000 men came the next year, and then 52,000 the next! In 1996, more than 1 million men in 23 stadium events, and hundreds of thousands more in "wake-up calls" and church seminars, stood up to be counted for Christ. Additionally, men's ministries in the local church are exploding!

Why has Promise Keepers been so successful in challenging men to take active steps toward growth in Christ? In large part, we believe it's because of the masculine context that surrounds the stadium event—and that you should factor into your small group as well.

THE MASCULINE CONTEXT OF LEARNING

 At Promise Keeper conferences, the interactions are masculine, the way the men sing is masculine, the way they respond to the invitation is masculine, and in that environment their hearts open up.

Those same men may have been passive in their faith and even passive at home or at church. Yet at Promise Keepers, they walk into a stadium or basketball arena and are soon doing the "wave"; shouting, "We love Jesus, yes we do, we love Jesus, how about you?"; and crying and praying openly with men who were strangers or just acquaintances moments before.

That's not to say that women can't be inspired to grow at an all-female event, nor that men and women can't grow together. But there does seem to be a unique environment that supports openness, seriousness, and spiritual strength in men over the long haul.

In a world that says there are no significant differences between men and women other than the physical, the fact remains that there are! And if there's a "new wine" effect of Promise Keepers, it was and is the masculine context.

Webster's dictionary tells us that a context is the environment in which something appears or exists. It then follows that a Christian masculine context is the environment in which Christian men can feel safe and keep their promises.

What is this context that will help you and your fellow group members to grow in Christ? Let's look at four key elements.

THE FIRST ELEMENT

Men need closeness, but they tend to view space as safety and intimacy as a threat or loss of power.

Promise Keepers works with thousands of men in large and small groups, and they consistently display the tendency to want some distance between themselves and others, especially other men. Additionally, distance is a key way men cope with stress. They become increasingly focused and withdrawn when problems are encountered in life.

Several years ago, I read a study that was done on the entering class of a major university. All the incoming men and women were given a written test that they were told would rate their literary skills. Actually, it was to assess differences between the sexes.

Each student was shown a picture of a young man and a young woman, sitting under a shade tree in the summer. Nearby, a beautiful stream flowed, and the grass was green. It was a beautiful pastoral view. The students' assignment: Write a short, imaginative essay describing what was happening in the scene.

The result: Almost unanimously, the women wrote about a couple in love who had found the time to get away to the countryside and enjoy the day together. Some of the men wrote along the same lines, but *more than half* described something far different. What they saw in the picture was violence.

Typical excerpts read, "There was this couple having a good time together, when suddenly, over that hill a group of bikers rode up . . ."; "Ninja turtles suddenly jumped out of the trees, and I had to fight them off . . ."

The conclusion of the study: Women look at a picture of closeness and feel positive about it. Men see a picture of closeness and are often frightened by it.

Consider the way men and women solve problems. Research shows that a woman feels better by talking about her problems with others, while a man feels better by acting on them. And the way a man goes about solving his problems is often by distancing himself and giving himself some time to process.

Typically, a man will "distance" himself from his spouse or others when:

- He needs to think about a problem and find a practical solution.
- He doesn't have an answer to a question or a problem.
- He has become upset or stressed.
- He feels a loss of direction or purpose.

"Distancing," then, is a common male trait. Yet we know from the Scriptures and from seeing it firsthand that men also need closeness. "As iron sharpens iron, so one man sharpens another" (Proverbs 27:17). American men must be convinced that nonsexual closeness with another man, as well as looking to another man for help, is positive and beneficial, not unmasculine. How can this happen in your small group and church?

Only by being told about it and by *seeing* the difference in other men's lives will a man be willing to develop trust and overcome his fear of closeness.

Therefore, we recommend you do the following:

First, model male closeness in your group by (a) starting where a man is and beginning to develop trust, and by (b) having men ready to offer contact and support, but not to overwhelm or threaten the men who visit your small group or ministry.

Second, communicate a close relationship's essential nature, and present it as a challenge. Do studies of key male friendships in the Bible. Dare men to take the first step in starting a relationship.

Third, choose meeting areas that work to your advantage. For example, if you expect 50 men to come, choose a room designed for about 75. Arrange the room with enough space between chairs so that each man is not overly threatened, but not with so much space as to be a gulf that must be transcended. For a small group, this may mean meeting at a friendly restaurant, or in a home or office where there's room to be comfortable.

Distance may be a cultural norm, but most men really want the closeness of strong male relationships.

THE SECOND ELEMENT

Most men communicate that they're listening by asking questions and offering solutions.

By nature, men are problem solvers who like to ask questions and give suggestions. (Just ask your wife if she thinks that statement is true!) Often a man will listen to his wife trying to express her feelings about something, and within moments he has asked several questions and proposed a solution. End of conversation!

The same thing will be true in your small group or men's ministry. Men are looking for the chance to offer their thoughts and observations, and even solutions to things they see as problems.

When working with men, then, remember to ask open-ended questions that encourage them to progressively share their lives. Men respond to a question only when the one asking is listening and interested in their answers. So the questioner has to value and understand listening. He has to get past focusing on what he's going to say next and focus instead on what the other men are saying.

Also ask process-producing, thought-stimulating questions. For instance, Jesus asked the disciples, "Who do men say I am?" When they had thought about that and answered, He took them a step deeper in the process: "Who do *you* say I am?"

Start general, and move to the specific. For many men, the competitive or defensive radar pops up when they're asked a pointed question. For example, "When was the last time you struggled with lust?" is a good question to get to in your group. But starting with general questions like "Why do you feel television is so slanted toward sex these days?" can warm men up to the subject instead of putting them on the immediate defensive.

Give processing time, and solicit feedback. We've all seen someone who asks a question—and then answers it before anyone else can! In Proverbs, we're told that's foolishness. "He who answers before listening—that is his folly and his shame" (18:13). It's important to give processing time when you ask questions. A little tension might be felt during the silence, but allowing others to frame their answer and listening well are important nonetheless.

Dr. Gary Rosberg heads a tremendous men's ministry in Des Moines, Iowa. More than 400 men gather each week for his meetings, and new chapters are beginning across the country. (I was so impressed by what Gary is doing that I started one at my home church in Phoenix.)

What makes this ministry so powerful in the lives of the men who attend? *Gary understands the masculine context.* The group meets once a week in the morning, and before the meeting there are lots of donuts, hot coffee, and good-natured conversation. Then the one-hour meeting time is broken into 20-minute segments. For 20 minutes, the men praise God in song and prayer; for 20 minutes, someone teaches; and for 20 minutes, the men meet in small groups.

Gary is a tremendous teacher. But as I've talked with many of the men in his group, I've learned that it's the small-group interaction they crave. That segment of each meeting is a time of asking and answering questions, offering a scripture that might be helpful, or simply stopping to pray for a man on the spot. Their meeting is held in a large room with movable chairs that allow the men to have some distance between each other yet still talk together, ask questions, and offer solutions.

THE THIRD ELEMENT

Most men are motivated by challenges and competition.

Achieving goals is important to men because it's a way for them to prove their competence and thus feel good about themselves. They feel even better if they achieve these goals on their own (so they know they weren't handed anything but earned their success).

That's why this book centers on helping men develop a plan of action and goals to shoot for in their spiritual and family lives. It fulfills the need of most men to have a plan they can work on and goals they can achieve.

The Lord Jesus consistently set tasks and goals for the disciples—even ones beyond their immediate reach. Just think of His last words to them: "Therefore go and make disciples of all nations, baptizing them in the name of the Father and of the Son and of the Holy Spirit . . ." (Matthew 28:19). Talk about setting a lifetime goal in front of them!

Even Paul declared, "Brothers, I do not consider myself yet to have taken hold of it. But one thing I do: Forgetting what is behind and straining toward what is ahead, I press on toward the goal to win the prize for which God has called me heavenward in Christ Jesus" (Philippians 3:13-14).

In large part, that's why this workbook is full of forms to fill out, goals to set in specific areas, worksheets to complete and discuss, and times to reflect prayerfully on what has been gained and where you yet need work. We men respond to a challenge, and this book gives us one. In summary, then, this element of the masculine context assumes that:

- Men need to be challenged.
- Men respond to a clear goal.
- The goal must be the right size, large enough to stretch men but small enough so that, with God's help, they can achieve it.
- Those smaller goals (we call them "horizon points" in this book) point men to a larger goal (the lifelong process of becoming more like Jesus Christ).

THE FOURTH ELEMENT

Many men are looking for structure that allows freedom for creativity.

This element sounds like an oxymoron (like "jumbo shrimp" or "mild hot sauce"). But think about the way men play games. It's important to know the boundaries. (Otherwise, how would we know when we scored?) There's a finite amount of time allowed, and distances are marked off on a playing field. And even if it's a pickup game where the only rule is "no blood, no foul," there are still some rules. Yet having these "restrictions" gives rise to incredible creativity in how the game is played! In offensive football, for example, we've got everything from the straight "T" backfield, to the shotgun, to the triple option, to the "West Coast offense," and so on.

What that illustrates is that men want some structure in their times together, yet there needs to be freedom for thought and expression as well. Let's go back to Gary Rosberg's men's group. The men who show up for meetings know there's a set structure. Yet the music changes; the lesson topic and even the teacher may change; and sometimes they discuss a single question, while other times the discussion is more open-ended. There's great encouragement, creativity, and bonding between the men because they meet within a solid structure.

You likewise want clear structure in your small group and men's ministry, but you also want a flexible environment where many issues can be addressed. In short:

- Men need enough structure to bring order.
- Men must be allowed enough freedom to focus on relationships.

• It takes time spent together in nonthreatening environments to develop trust.

The four elements of the masculine context are keys to allowing your group to come close together and stay together as you face barriers and move toward God's best.

With this context in mind, let's move now to part two of the workbook and the actual process of designing your spiritual growth plan. (For more on this subject of how men learn and the masculine context for growth, see *Brothers!* by Geoff Gorsuch with Dan Schaffer.)

DISCUSSION QUESTIONS

1. Think about a time when you've experienced the masculine context discussed in this chapter (anything from sports teams, to school classes, to being in the service, to attending a men's retreat).

What are some distinct positives about gathering with men?

What are some negatives that could develop in an all-male gathering?

2. A key aspect of the masculine context is building trust with a man before offering advice. What does it take to build a bridge of trust with another man? Put another way, what could someone do to build a bridge of trust to you?

3. It's commonly said that men aren't as emotional as women. However, most men don't have any trouble expressing anger. Why do you think that is? What has helped you deal with anger?

Part II

The Making of a

purity
devotion
reconciliation
repentance

humility
servanthood
perseverance

GODLY MAN

CREATING
YOUR PLAN

Chapter 5

MOVING

FORWARD BY

LOOKING BACK

The year was 1969, and Mike had been deep "in country" in Vietnam for four months. In the space of 120 days, he'd gone from a "new guy" to an old-timer in his 183rd Airborne company, which had already seen numerous casualties.

Back in Advanced Infantry Training and Airborne school, he'd applied himself wholeheartedly to the physical conditioning, weapons, and tactics he was taught. "I thought those things would be important when I got to 'the Nam,'" he says. But at the same time, he struggled mightily with something he didn't think was nearly as important—map reading. "I was a lowly private and wanted to stay that way," he explains. "I figured the squad leaders and sergeants were the ones primarily responsible for calling in air strikes. They kept telling us that map reading was important. But I didn't think it was that big a deal for me to know."

Now four months had gone by in Vietnam, and as he and his squad were on a daylight patrol, they came under heavy fire from a large hutch several hundred yards away. The first burst of fire struck down his squad leader, and suddenly, Mike was the senior man. As such, responsibility for calling in air evac or artillery support rested on him.

With fire raking their position, he keyed the radio and was told that air support wasn't available quickly, but artillery support was. He knew just what to do; he'd watched his sergeant do it a dozen times. He called for the artillery adviser to "walk in" a series of rounds from behind the target. He was sure the coordinates he gave the officer would have the first rounds land approximately 150 yards beyond the target. Then they'd drop to 100 yards, then 50, allowing him to correct for distance and accuracy until the shells were landing right on top of the enemy and the artillery could fire for effect.

However, while he knew *what* to do and where he wanted the rounds to go, *he'd blown one important step.* Mike hadn't judged accurately his position on the map.

He and his squad heard the first round scream overhead. But instead of landing behind the hutch that was his target, the shells landed just 100 yards in front of his own position! Instantly he knew that the next round would be only 50 yards in front of him, and the third round would fall right on top of him! He screamed into the mike for the artillery to cease fire!

Thankfully, the adviser was listening and adjusted the next salvo to go *away* from Mike's position and toward the enemy. When the next barrage hit 50 yards in front of the Viet Cong, they abandoned their positions and ran. It was a good thing for them, because the next set of shells came in right on target, obliterating the hutch.

When reinforcements arrived, all his company commander said to Mike was, "Good job, private. Walking the rounds in the way you did was unusual, but it showed good thinking. The enemy sure seemed surprised!"

Actually, they weren't as surprised as Mike had been!

Mike's goal had been clear in his mind. But because he hadn't been sure of where he was on the map, he couldn't hit the target. And the same thing is true in our "hitting the target" when it comes to our spiritual growth.

PINPOINTING YOUR SPIRITUAL POSITION

 We've already stated that the goal of this workbook and of Promise Keepers is that men become more like Jesus Christ. Beginning with the next chapter, you'll be encouraged to zero in on seven specific aspects of a godly life (the seven promises of a Promise Keeper). However, to make sure you "hit the target," it's important to identify accurately your present position—to see where God has brought you and where you are today. That pinpointing process is important for your small group as well.

In this chapter, you'll find two self-assessment tools to fill out and share with your small group (and with your spouse if you're married). They'll give you and your group a visual picture of your present spiritual position, and they'll also provide important information about who you are and where you've been.

The "High Point/Trial Point" form comes first. It's a graphic way of capturing some of the strengths and struggles, the high points and difficult challenges, that have shaped your life. The second is a "Past- or Future-Based" inventory based on the promise of Jeremiah 29:11: "'For I know the plans I have for you,' declares the LORD, 'plans to prosper you and not to harm you, plans to give you hope and a future.'"

In the process of filling out these forms and sharing your personal history with your small group, two important things will take place.

MORE THAN A HISTORY LESSON

First, you'll be surprised at what you learn about those in your group—even men you may have known for years. That's because it's easy to think that being around someone is the same as really knowing him, and it isn't.

In the weeks to come, we think you'll gain more from this small-group experience than from any you've been in before. But that won't happen if the sharing level never gets deeper than "exchanging the weather report":

"How're you doing?"
"Great! How're you doing?"
"Great!"

Filling out these forms provides a great ice-breaker as you begin your group. It can help you explain who you are and where God has taken you. In fact, describing your high points and trial points is one way of giving a pictorial testimony.

A particular trial point may have been the very thing God used to bring you to Christ (e.g., "We had a child who faced some difficult physical challenges, yet through that experience, we came to know Christ"). For others, a high point may signal the culmination of years of hard work or even the answer to years of prayer (e.g., "After 20 years of my wife praying for me, God finally broke down my pride, and I went to church, where I came to know Jesus Christ"). One of the most encouraging things you can do is to explain how God brought you to Himself, and the first form can help you do just that.

Second, discussing these forms with your small group can become a loving accountability tool. As we saw in the last chapter, Proverbs tells us, "As iron sharpens iron, so one man sharpens another" (Proverbs 27:17). Giving the men in your group a picture of where you've been and where you are today in relation to the promise of Jeremiah 29:11 provides a positive tool for encouraging growth and facing challenges.

To illustrate the first tool we want you to fill out, let's look at the lives of three men who may be familiar to you.

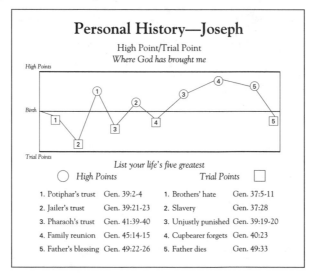

That form captures the patriarch Joseph's high points and trial points. Outside of the Lord Jesus Himself, no person in Scripture displayed as many Christlike traits as Joseph. He was tempted to sin by Potiphar's wife (as Jesus was tempted by Satan), yet he always resisted. Joseph could have condemned those who sought to take his life, but like Jesus, he chose to forgive them. In fact, throughout his life, you see a pattern of consistent spiritual trust and growth, with even the low points he faced being caused by living in a fallen world, not by his own sin.

As you fill out your form, perhaps you, like Joseph, grew up knowing God and have matured steadily in Him throughout your life. That's great! Not that you're perfect in any way, nor that you've had as many dramatic opportunities to trust God as Joseph did. But an overall look at your life story reflects a consistency of spiritual growth, and most of the trials you've faced have come from living in a fallen world instead of from falling yourself.

Perhaps, however, your life story is more like that of a man named David. Take a look at his high points and trial points and you'll see deep lows and high highs.

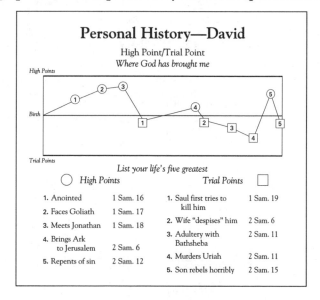

Yes, those are the high points and challenge points of King David. His life of faith looks like an EKG readout! You see high highs, like his great victories of faith in defeating Goliath and in bringing the Ark of the Covenant back to Jerusalem. Yet you also see deep, dramatic lows, like his fall into sin with Bathsheba and even plotting the murder of Uriah the Hittite. Not only that, but the trial points David faced weren't primarily a reflection of his living in a fallen world. Instead, they were the negative consequences of his own sinful actions, like having a son rebel and try to take his life!

As you look at your life story, do you see a yo-yo ride of faith and falling? Do you see times of great spiritual strength, but also experiences of stinging personal failure? If so, you share something in common with David, and you have something important to share with your group.

Joseph trusted God throughout his life, and David loved God yet had a series of personal highs and lows. Jonah depicts a third life pattern. That's the person who was once running from the Lord but later sought to live a life of faith.

Almost all of us have heard the story of Jonah, the reluctant prophet, since we were children. Every man since Adam has tried to "hide" from God at some time and in some way; for some men, Jonah's story comes too close for comfort to mirroring their own.

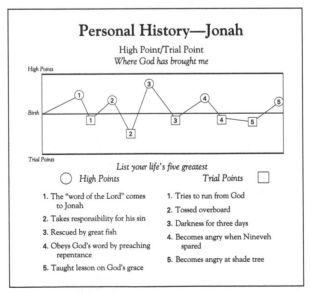

Personal History—Jonah

High Point/Trial Point
Where God has brought me

List your life's five greatest

○ High Points   Trial Points □

High Points

1. The "word of the Lord" comes to Jonah
2. Takes responsibility for his sin
3. Rescued by great fish
4. Obeys God's word by preaching repentance
5. Taught lesson on God's grace

Trial Points

1. Tries to run from God
2. Tossed overboard
3. Darkness for three days
4. Becomes angry when Nineveh spared
5. Becomes angry at shade tree

The story of Jonah begins with his actively running from God. Yet Jonah ran into the truth King David captured years earlier in a song: "Where can I go from your Spirit? Where can I flee from your presence? If I go up to the heavens, you are there; if I make my bed in the depths, you are there. If I rise on the wings of the dawn, if I settle on the far side of the sea, even there your hand will guide me, your right hand will hold me fast" (Psalm 139:7-10).

Perhaps Jonah would never have tried to run from God if he'd read David's words—but I have my doubts. Jonah was dead set on disobeying God and getting as far from Him as possible. Yet in spite of what he wanted, God caught him and brought him back to his senses and Himself.

Perhaps you feel a bit like a Jonah as you enter this group experience. Maybe you've come reluctantly to Christ, or very late in life. Perhaps you were "tossed overboard" by a loved one or friend and sank lower in your life than ever before, but God graciously rescued you and gave you a renewed or newfound faith.

As you fill out your "High Point/Trial Point" form with five of each kind of "point," if you feel it shows a pattern like Jonah's, don't despair. You couldn't have come up on shore at a better place. In a small group of committed Christian men, you'll find both God's love and acceptance *and* the encouragement to get up off the beach and set about His work.

AN IMPORTANT NOTE BEFORE FILLING OUT YOUR FORMS

We've mentioned time and again that spiritual growth is best accomplished in the context of a small group of supportive friends, and also with your spouse if you're married. Let's put some teeth in those assumptions before we go any further.

For example, how would you like to lower the stress level in your life, significantly increase your resistance to colds and sickness, and actually live longer as a result? No, the answer isn't a magic vitamin supplement. Rather, it's staying involved in your small group.

Those are just some of the many benefits clinical studies show come from being in a small group. Others include greater motivation to face and break negative habits, the opportunity to learn new coping and caring skills, and a place where people do more than just *know* your name—they *pray for you* by name.

For those men who are married, we strongly urge you to share with your wife the work you do in this workbook. An ideal way to go through this study would be to read a chapter yourself, filling out the evaluation tools and exercises. Then, even before you go to your group meeting, discuss your evaluation and prayerful projections with your spouse. (Be careful, however, not to burden her with information that would hurt her unnecessarily.)

Your wife's role isn't to be your policeman or an uncaring "editor," but rather to be a loving and honest encourager. Actively asking for and getting her feedback, insight, and encouragement on each aspect of your plan is crucial to seeing your family move forward. And working through your plan with her doesn't negate your leadership in the home, it demonstrates it.

Even if your wife "sees" something differently from you or gives you a lower evaluation number in some area than you gave yourself, don't become defensive. Honor her as a joint heir of life (see 1 Peter 3:7). Not only that, but realize that as your helpmate, she can offer her unique perspective on your life, marriage, fathering, and background. Remember that "fools despise wisdom and discipline" (Proverbs 1:7), but wise men welcome them.

Personal History

High Point/Trial Point
Where God has brought me

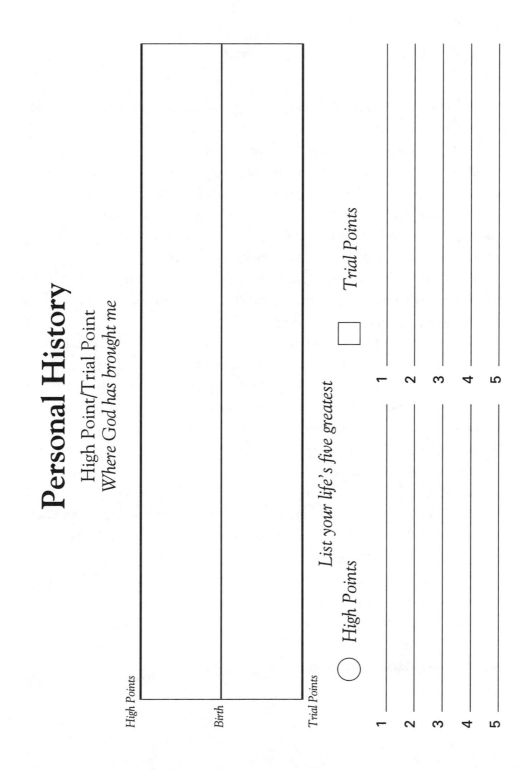

High Points

Birth

Trial Points

List your life's five greatest

○ High Points

1 _____
2 _____
3 _____
4 _____
5 _____

☐ Trial Points

1 _____
2 _____
3 _____
4 _____
5 _____

Now that you've filled out this form, take a look at a related tool. It asks you to evaluate, on a 1 to 10 scale, where you are in being either future-based or past-based in your core beliefs and actions.

This tool grows out of the promise of Jeremiah 29:11, which was quoted earlier. The apostle Paul, even when he was writing from a Roman prison, had a hopeful future and a forward focus. He told us, "Not that I have already obtained all this, or have already been made perfect, but I press on to take hold of that for which Christ Jesus took hold of me" (Philippians 3:12).

It's not that remembering isn't important. In fact, more than 100 times in the Old Testament (more than 60 times in the Psalms alone!), we're told to remember. Yet we're not to be stuck in the past.

Right now, as you look at your life, it's time to ask yourself a hard question: Do you tend, by your everyday actions and attitudes, to be past- or future-based? Was there an experience, or a series of experiences, that convinced you your best days are behind you; that whatever you might have had to contribute was somehow lost in the past; or that "if only" something in the past had happened or not happened, everything would be different in your life?

Or do you see a future that offers the opportunity to change? Do you believe that effort, even if it doesn't bring immediate recognition or advancement, will still be counted? Are you confident that hurts can be taken before the Lord, and that even "family ghosts" and painful failures can be forgotten? ("As far as the east is from the west . . ." [Psalm 103:12].)

Below is the self-evaluation tool. If 10 represents a decidedly future-based orientation to life (a Jeremiah 29:11 attitude of a bright, hopeful future), and 1 represents the feeling that you're deeply stuck in the past (or in past failures), put a mark where you are today. (For greater insight, have two people who know you well give you a rating, too.)

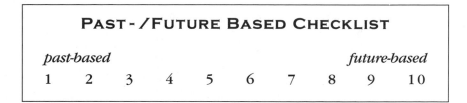

LOOKING BACK TO UNDERSTAND AND ENCOURAGE EACH OTHER

Take one or two group meetings after completing these forms to go through each person's responses. With a clear picture of where you and your group have been, and how positively focused on the future you all are, you're ready to develop your spiritual plan of action.

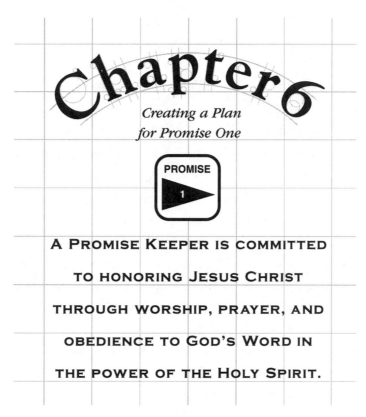

Chapter 6

*Creating a Plan
for Promise One*

PROMISE 1

A PROMISE KEEPER IS COMMITTED TO HONORING JESUS CHRIST THROUGH WORSHIP, PRAYER, AND OBEDIENCE TO GOD'S WORD IN THE POWER OF THE HOLY SPIRIT.

 Core issue: intimacy with God
Key passage for your group to review: Psalm 73:25

---

alk about a biting lesson!

A few milleniums ago, God gave a wandering group of Israelites a vivid (and unusual) lesson about where life begins and ends. It seems that even after Moses had parted the Red Sea by God's power and led a captive nation out of bondage, the people continually sinned by grumbling nonstop against the Lord.

They grumbled about His miraculous provision of bread because He hadn't provided meat to go along with it. They grumbled about the heat and not having enough water, and they grumbled against God's designated leader. Finally, God deemed their sin to be so serious that He passed judgment against their lack of gratitude and rejection of His guidance.

In Numbers 21, we read that He sent "fiery serpents" into their midst—poisonous, slithering agents of punishment. To be bitten by one of these serpents meant a painful, certain death. The people ran to Moses and asked if he would petition God for a way of escape from this sentence of being snakebit.

In a gracious act of love for the same people who had heaped scorn on him, that's exactly what Moses did. He went before Almighty God, begging Him to provide a way of escape. God mercifully answered his prayer. But He provided an unusual means of deliverance.

"The LORD said to Moses, 'Make a snake and put it up on a pole; anyone who is bitten can look at it and live.' So Moses made a bronze snake and put it up on a pole. Then when anyone was bitten by a snake and looked at the bronze snake, he lived" (21:8-9).

What does this story have to do with promise one, a call to be fully committed to Jesus Christ? No doubt you've heard the words of John 3:16: "For God so loved the world that he gave his one and only Son, that whoever believes in him shall not perish but have eternal life."

But can you quote John 3:*14-15?* There Jesus, explaining to Nicodemus who He was, told him, "Just as Moses lifted up the snake in the desert, so the Son of Man must be lifted up, that everyone who believes in him may have eternal life."

Long ago in the desert, God provided a way of escape. Everyone who had been bitten had only one option: Look up to a single source of healing that God alone had provided.

They couldn't cure themselves by their own self-effort, willful sacrifice, material substance, or massive intellect. It took a simple act of faith to "look up" at God's provision. (Literally, they were looking up at a snake lashed to a tribal standard carrier—a long pole with a crossbeam—*a cross!*)

Can you see now why Jesus used that event in the desert, and the graphic picture it conveyed, to explain to a questioning Nicodemus who He was? He was God's own Son who would be lifted up on a cross. And when He was, He would draw all men to Himself and provide the only way of escape from a "snakebitten" world, condemned and dying of sin.

That's why the first promise of a promise keeper is to honor Jesus Christ as our Lord and Savior. He alone, fully God and fully man, has faced every temptation we've faced, yet without sin. He alone was the culmination of the Law and the prophets, the one angels longed to see, the Eternal Word of God made flesh, and the author and perfecter of our faith. He alone took our punishment for sin upon Himself when He was lifted up. And looking up to Him is the only way of escaping death and finding the narrow way to everlasting life that God has provided.

For these and endless volumes of reasons more, He alone is worthy of our praise, our lives, our all. As men of God, we seek to reflect our commitment to Jesus Christ in faith and action in at least three ways.

1. We worship Him.

What does it mean to worship the Lord? In England, the story is told of an agnostic art critic who went to a noted church to view a new statue of Jesus. He stood at the back of the church, singularly unimpressed with what he saw, making notes for what would be a scathing newspaper review.

That's when the church custodian saw him observing the statue and walked over to him. "Sir," he told the skeptic, "you're in the wrong place."

"No, I'm not," the man protested, explaining that he was there to view the new statue.

"Please," the custodian insisted, "come with me. You're in the wrong place." And he led the man to a place right in front of the statue of Jesus and had him get down on his knees. From that vantage point, looking up from his knees, the critic saw the way the sculptor had fashioned this masterpiece to be viewed.

Worshiping the Lord means looking up to Him in faith, thanking Him for what He alone has done, praising Him with our whole heart, word, and song. (As a part of each promise cycle you'll go through with your small group in this workbook, one week is set aside for you to gather and worship the Lord.)

2. We pray.

A second outworking of a sold-out commitment to Jesus Christ is consistent prayer. For a godly man, prayer isn't elective but required.

Today, global positioning satellites can relay information to a hand-held device and tell you, within a meter, your location on planet earth. That's impressive technology. But for those who want clear guidance for their lives; wisdom for their days; and the opportunity to share the hurts, needs, dreams, and goals of their hearts, that comes from a daily commitment to prayer. In addition, prayer can help a man "guard his heart" and keep bitterness, anger, and other relationship-killers from taking root in his life.

Daily face-to-face conversation with our loving Lord and heavenly Father can make all the difference in becoming a godly man.

3. We obey God's Word.

Several years ago, Billy Graham recounted an incident that happened while he was traveling on an airplane. The man in the seat directly in front of him had been drinking before he got on the plane. Already tipsy, he became incensed when the stewardess refused to serve him any more alcohol.

He filled the air with profanities until the flight attendant, in an attempt to calm him down, said, "Sir, do you know who is sitting right behind you? It's Billy Graham."

Instantly the man turned around and said, "Oh, Dr. Graham! What an honor to meet you! I went to one of your crusades, and it changed my life!"

Right. He may have felt something change, but what a plane full of people around him saw and heard was coarse talk and godless behavior.

Obedience to Almighty God doesn't mean we slavishly keep a set of rules in an attempt to gain His favor or our salvation. We are "saved through faith . . . not by works, so that no one can boast" (Ephesians 2:8-9). Yet out of love for the God who redeemed us, we seek to live in a way that reflects the life and love of Jesus Christ. That's why obedience begins by knowing and seeking to keep His Word (like the description of a godly man in Psalm 15).

A godly man seeks by his daily actions, not just his words, to reflect the love of Christ to his family, workplace, community, and world.

Let's end this summary of promise one the way we began . . . *Looking up.*

In a crazy world filled with sin, corruption, and compromise, life only makes sense when we forsake our pride and look up to a sovereign, almighty, loving God.

LIVING IT OUT

"You may have lymphoma, Bud," the grim-faced doctor said. "I'd like to refer you to a cancer specialist at Cedars-Sinai Medical Center in Los Angeles."

Bud Schaedel was one of those people who had been blessed with lifelong good health. On rare occasions he caught some kind of bug, but he never let it slow him down or even force him to miss a day of work.

Right after Christmas 1989, however, Bud came down with the flu, and a week or so later he noticed swelling in the glands along his neck. Then came the terrible diagnosis.

Bud appeared outwardly unfazed by the news, but his wife, Connie, barely kept her composure in the doctor's office. Before Connie and Bud met, they had both known the pain and frustration of a failed marriage relationship.

Perhaps because he was determined to have a better marriage and be a better husband than he had been the first time around, Bud never quit treating Connie like a queen. Over the years, his constant supply of unconditional love mended wounds she thought would never be closed. "His love was an unspeakable gift to me," she says.

Yet Bud and Connie's idyllic world seemed ready to collapse around them that day in the doctor's office. But that wasn't the end of Bud's story—just the beginning.

Bud had gone through a long period of spiritual drifting. But now, suddenly faced with cancer's undeniable reminder of his mortality, Bud evidenced a growing spiritual hunger.

In the winter of 1991, the lymphoma flared up and the doctors began the first round of chemotherapy. That was also when Bud and Connie found an outstanding church to attend. The more spiritual food he devoured, the hungrier Bud seemed for more. For the first time in his life, he began listening to a Christian radio station as he drove to and from work. It was there, in the spring of 1993, that he first heard about something called a Promise Keepers conference.

Late that spring, Bud casually asked one of the church staff members what he knew about Promise Keepers and its upcoming conference. The man's face lit up, his eyes zeroed in on Bud's, and he said, "I've been looking for someone interested enough to attend the conference and then take the lead in finding ways to get the men of our church involved in Promise Keepers."

Bud literally backed away, held up a hand, and said, "Hey, I was just asking! I'm really too busy to consider going."

But eventually, Bud agreed to attend the conference with his brother-in-law Larry. He and Larry joined 50,000 other men at the University of Colorado football stadium, in a blistering sun and scorching 104-degree heat, for the two-day conference.

Larry was concerned about how the brutal heat might affect Bud. But throughout the conference, Bud seemed oblivious to any physical discomfort, perhaps because he was so excited about what he found himself a part of. From the opening words of the conference, Bud was totally absorbed. On Friday night, when speaker Greg Laurie challenged the men to be sure they were trusting in Jesus as their Savior, as Bud listened, he realized, *I've never done that. In all these years of going to church, reading the Bible, and everything else, I've never really given my life to Christ. I need to do that, and tonight's the night! Thank You, Lord!*

A few minutes later, when Laurie asked the men who wanted to commit their lives to Christ to come down in front of the stage, Bud turned to Larry and said with conviction, "I need to go down there."

Laurie asked the throng of men to kneel as he led them in a prayer of confession and commitment. Bud knelt with the others, quietly repeating Laurie's prayer even as he thought, *This is the best thing I've ever done. I've never been so sure of what I needed to do.*

That was only the beginning of Bud's transformation that weekend. He caught the first glimpse of what God just might be able to do through him.

More men from our church have got to come here next year, Bud thought. *If I tell them what God has done for me this weekend, they'll want to come, and He'll get a hold of them the way He's doing for me.* His goal would be to recruit as many men as possible to attend a Promise Keepers conference already scheduled for Anaheim the next spring.

Bud immediately set about living up to the commitments he'd made to God and to himself in Boulder. He clearly intended to be a true man of God, and nothing was going to stop him.

At every possible opportunity in church, Bud wanted to talk about Promise Keepers and the upcoming conference. In one men's meeting, someone said, "Wouldn't it be great if we could get 50 men to go?"

Bud's response was, "Surely we can do better than that!"

"What about 100 men?" another proposed.

"No, higher!" Bud urged.

The agreed-upon target was eventually 150 men. But everyone got the idea that Bud wouldn't be satisfied until every man in church had signed up. Sometimes it seemed he was out to recruit the entire world.

Then, during the fall of 1993, Bud's lymphoma returned. This was much sooner than his doctors had expected. Another round of chemo began in January 1994.

Through the entire ordeal, Bud continued to recruit more people for the Anaheim conference in May. To enable some men to go who couldn't afford the registration fee, the Schaedels set up a scholarship fund.

As Bud intensified his efforts to sign up more men for the Promise Keepers conference, the chemo began to take its toll on his health, and he took a rapid turn for the worse. Bud ended up in the hospital, and the seriousness of his situation was clear to anyone who walked into his room. For those visitors who had last seen him at church or at work just the week before, his sudden deterioration was shocking. Yet his spirits remained high. When someone commented about how hard life can be, Bud responded, "Life isn't so hard. It's just a boot camp for heaven." And he continued to talk to visitors about Promise Keepers.

Bud's breathing became so labored that he was moved to intensive care and put on a respirator. Once the tube was inserted down his throat, there was no more talking for Bud. He had to resort to communicating by touch. But when the president of the church's men's group arrived that night, Bud excitedly held up 10 fingers. Connie had to interpret: "Bud wants to tell you that we've decided to fund 10 scholarships to the Promise Keepers conference. So on Sunday he wants you to announce that there's no reason for anyone to decide he can't afford to go."

That was Bud's last message to the world outside his family. He had done all he could to give as many men as possible the opportunity to experience Promise Keepers. By Friday morning, he was no longer conscious. And in the early hours of Saturday morning, Bud Schaedel died.

Just two weeks later, in the closing session of the conference in Anaheim Stadium, Bud's pastor, Lee Eliason, was called to the platform. He told the men filling the "Big A" about coming to know Bud Schaedel, a man whose life had been changed at the Boulder conference less than a year before. He spoke movingly about the impact Bud's love and support had had on him and his ministry.

Then Lee directed everyone's attention to a specific spot in the upper deck and asked the *250* men from Bud's church to stand in honor of the man who had worked so hard for them to attend.

That night, the men in Anaheim heard Bud's widow speak, too.

"Gentlemen," she said, "I just want you all to know . . . it works. Amazing grace fell on Bud last summer in Boulder. And it will fall on you."

MAKING YOUR PLAN

Congratulations! You're ready to begin a process of spiritual goal-setting that we pray will bless your life and the lives of your family and generations yet to come!

To illustrate how to work through the forms at the end of this chapter and in the six that follow and develop your plan, let's look at a hypothetical group of men, and one man in particular, to demonstrate the process. (As always, feel free to modify the process to meet your unique needs.)

Following One Promise Keeper's Steps

Don went to a Promise Keepers conference for the first time this past summer, and it so changed him that he went back to his church and became an active part of its new men's ministry. He also accepted the challenge to join a small group with Joe, Jeff, and Jim. Their assignment: go through this workbook together. Let's watch how he and they did just that.

Don and the men in his group picked a time (7:00 A.M. on Tuesdays) and a place (the church) to meet each week. They also committed to working through this workbook together and coming up with a specific, prayed-over spiritual growth plan.

THEIR FIRST FOUR WEEKS

For the first four weeks, they worked through the first four chapters of this workbook, one chapter per meeting. Each man read through the appropriate chapter ahead of time, and then in their meeting they used the discussion questions at the end of the chapter to stimulate their conversation and gain a fuller understanding of the principles found there.

WEEK FIVE

Next, they read chapter 5 and filled in and discussed with each other the two personal history forms found there. Don had never been in a small group before, and seeing the high points and trial points of the other men's lives was a great experience. He saw clearly that each man desired to grow in Christ and that, like him, none of them was perfect.

WEEK SIX

As a homework assignment before their next meeting, Don and the others read the brief overview of promise one that's found in this chapter and the story of how one man tried to live it out.

Then they began the first draft of their spiritual growth plan by completing the three forms found later in this chapter. These forms are titled "Personal

Evaluation Point," "Setting a Prayerful Horizon," and "Action Plan Worksheet."

Don read the material and filled out all three forms on promise one *before* his group meeting. Together, these forms gave Don a "baseline" measure of where he was today, as well as an initial plan for where he'd like to be in three years.

To demonstrate how to fill out each of these forms, let's look at Don's.

Filling Out His Personal Evaluation Point

Don asked himself four important questions in determining his personal evaluation point for promise one:

> 1. Have I demonstrated *consistency* in living out what I know to be God's best in this promise area?
> 2. Have I been *committed to growth* in this area?
> 3. Have I been *open to correction* when I haven't measured up in this area?
> 4. *Do important others* (e.g., my wife) see the same consistency, commitment, and openness to correction that I do?

In short, he looked at how consistently he's now living out this first promise to honor God above all else—not how well he did *last* year or where he *should* be, but where he is today. Then he asked himself how actively he'd sought to learn and grow in this area, and if he'd been "defensive" or willing to accept counsel or correction as needed.

Answering those questions as honestly and objectively as he could, Don gave himself a preliminary evaluation point of 6 in this first promise area. He felt he had worked hard at being a committed Christian, yet his prayer life and lack of knowledge of God's Word presented a "gap" he wanted to close.

Then, as a reality check and reflection point, he asked someone important to him—in this case, his wife—to give him a mark as well. She gave him an 8 because of his consistency in attending church and urging her and the kids to be there as well, and because of the way he had started to have personal devotions since his weekend at the Promise Keepers conference.

Based on his own reflection and that feedback from someone who knew him well, Don revised his first personal evaluation point and settled on a 7 (see below).

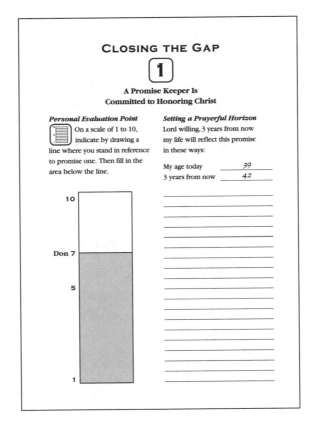

Completing His Prayerful Horizon Form

Don then moved to write out and picture a prayerful horizon. The goal of this form is to have you look beyond where you are today to where you could be by God's grace and significant effort at a specific point in the future (a pattern you can follow for the rest of your life). For our purposes in this book, the horizon point is *three years from now*. This prayerful horizon gives you a target for spiritual growth.

This form provides a picture that isn't bound by "whys" or "what ifs." It's written independent of obstacles like "I don't have any spare time," "I've started and given up on a dozen goals in the past," or "I've never been to Bible school." It's simply a prayerful opportunity for you to say, "Lord, You know where I am today. I want to live for You. Here's what I'd like my life to reflect three years from now as You give me life and strength. I'm open to counsel and, most of all, to the direction of Your Word and Spirit. Please direct me toward Your best in this area."

As Don turned his attention to completing his prayerful horizon form, he organized his thoughts and penciled in a rough draft on a separate sheet of paper. Then he showed his horizon form to his wife and a close friend before discussing it with his small group. Here's his initial prayerful horizon:

Promise One
Setting a Prayerful Horizon

Three years from now, Lord willing, I'll be 42 years old. There are several ways I'd like to reflect this promise and be more like Jesus. I know I need to be more of a man of prayer. I do pray for my wife and children at odd times and most days. But at my horizon point three years from now, I'd like to be praying with my wife at night, on our knees, before we go to bed. And I'd like to be asking my kids each day for something I could pray about for them, and then purposefully do that.

I'd also be more of a man of God's Word. I've done pretty well in reading through the Bible with that devotional guide. However, I sometimes feel I'm just reading a chapter to meet my daily goal, not because I need His Word daily. My prayer is that at the three-year horizon point, I'd have gone deeper in both knowing how to study God's Word and in digging into the riches there. For me, that means getting and using a study

> *Bible that can help me understand certain passages, and a Bible dictionary to look up key words that I really don't understand.*
>
> *Finally, I'd be more of a man of worship, particularly when things go wrong in my life. Right now, I tend to go it on my own or just ask God to "bail me out" when a problem hits. I don't think to praise Him or ask what He's trying to teach me through what's happened. Three years from now, I'd want to be the kind of man who doesn't just "react" when something negative happens. Instead of reacting in anger or jumping to my own solution, I want to be someone who slows down and asks the Lord, "What are You teaching me through this event or situation?" and "How can I praise You in spite of, or because of, it?"*

As you'll notice, this form is a general reflection on who Don would like to become in his relationship with Almighty God. It describes certain attitudes he'd like to see and actions that would mark him as someone who had "closed the gap" on being more like Jesus Christ.

Notice, too, that it took Don more than one pass to get a prayerful horizon on paper. Also, what he wrote didn't have to be typed out or grammatically correct. It didn't have to be four pages long or worthy of publication. But it should reflect his heart and where he wanted to go after prayerful reflection. Then, from this form, Don began to draw out his initial *specifics* that made up his plan of action.

Compiling His Action Plan Worksheet

It takes action—moving forward step by step—for a man to pick out a point on the horizon and reach it. To chart his course, Don now completed his first action plan worksheet.

Let's look at Don's sheet, and then at how he went about filling out the three parts found there.

First, Don wrote in three action steps drawn from his prayerful horizon sheet.

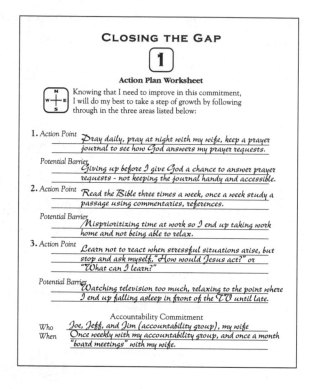

These are specific, positive, measurable actions or attitudes that he could put into practice daily or at least regularly. For Don, these included goals in relation to his prayer life, going deeper in God's Word, and reacting to trials in a godly way.

Then, referring back to the chapter on barriers (and reflecting on his own tendencies and life history), Don listed three potential barriers to living out his action steps. He knew these were things he had to talk about, perhaps even study or seek godly counsel for, if he was to move toward God's best. In his case, these included a fear of failure (because of a track record of starting but not finishing things), poor use of time at work (which meant bringing home work at night that consumed time he could otherwise spend on spiritual things), and late-night TV.

This third barrier referred to a bad habit he'd gotten into of "relaxing" in front of the TV after the late news. Because he felt he deserved some down time, he'd sit and watch a nightly talk show or movie. Unfortunately, instead of relaxing and going to bed with his wife as he should, he'd stumble into the bedroom long after she'd fallen asleep and wake up tired and grumpy the next morning.

By beginning the day worn out instead of rested, he felt he was handling the inevitable problems of the work day less effectively than he otherwise could. Instead of coming to work feeling centered in his faith and having prayed with his wife or read God's Word the night before, he felt anxious, on edge, and unprepared.

These action steps and potential barriers formed Don's first pass in developing a specific plan of action. Over the course of their small-group time, he knew these items could change as God impressed upon him a more important step or pointed out a more damaging barrier to confront. But he needed to start somewhere, and these initial steps and roadblocks to avoid were the things he discussed with his spouse and small group and asked them to pray about—and hold him accountable to.

> ***Please Note:*** If you've been keeping track, Don came up with three action steps and three potential barriers for just this first promise area. If you're thinking ahead, that means he'll have *21* action steps and *21* potential barriers that will make up his plan before he's done. Even if there's some duplication of steps or barriers (and duplication is fine), that could be as many as 40 different things to keep in mind! *But don't be overwhelmed.* Please keep reading and working to develop your plan.
>
> After creating your plan, you'll be cycling through one promise at a time for seven weeks at a stretch. And each week, you'll focus on just one exercise to help you go deeper in that promise. That's more than manageable as you seek to move toward God's best.

Finally, Don penciled in the names of the three other men in his small group as the ones who would provide the accountability commitment to help him live out his plan. Now he was ready to go on to the next chapter and read, evaluate, and form a plan of action for the second promise area.

YOUR TURN

That's a picture of how to fill out the three evaluation and planning forms in each chapter of this section. *It's your turn now.* What you come up with doesn't have to be profound, and it isn't something you're doing to "prove" something to anyone in your group. It's just a basic plan of action for a man who's in process, as we all are, but who wants to "close the gap" between where he is and where he wants to be and "go the distance" with his Lord.

After completing your forms, move your action plan into your daily planner/organizer. In Don's case, for example, he might schedule times for Bible study, and he might also plan dates with his wife and each of his children to tell them about his new commitments relative to them. You might want to make copies of the planning forms found throughout this workbook, reducing them as necessary to fit into your planner/organizer. (You have permission to make these copies for your personal use.)

CLOSING THE GAP

A Promise Keeper Is Committed to Honoring Christ

Personal Evaluation Point

On a scale of 1 to 10, indicate by drawing a line where you stand in reference to promise one. Then fill in the area below the line.

Setting a Prayerful Horizon

Lord willing, 3 years from now my life will reflect this promise in these ways:

My age today _____
3 years from now _____

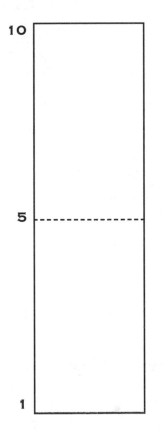

_____
_____
_____
_____
_____
_____
_____
_____
_____
_____
_____
_____
_____
_____
_____
_____
_____

Closing the Gap

Action Plan Worksheet

Knowing that I need to improve in this commitment, I will do my best to take a step of growth by following through in the three areas listed below:

1. *Action Point*

_____

_____

Potential Barrier

_____

_____

2. *Action Point*

_____

_____

Potential Barrier

_____

_____

3. *Action Point*

_____

_____

Potential Barrier

_____

_____

Accountability Commitment

Who _____

When _____

Now move your plan into the appropriate places in your daily planner.

Chapter 7

*Creating a Plan
for Promise Two*

PROMISE 2

A PROMISE KEEPER IS COMMITTED TO PURSUING VITAL RELATIONSHIPS WITH A FEW OTHER MEN, UNDERSTANDING THAT HE NEEDS BROTHERS TO HELP HIM KEEP HIS PROMISES.

Core issue: brotherhood

Key passage to review in your group: Hebrews 3:12-13

I didn't know my father well. He left the family when I was only two months old. When I finally met him years later, he was withdrawn and unwilling to say much about himself or his past. But one time he varied dramatically from his usual pattern of silence.

Back in 1969, my twin brother, Jeff, and I were getting ready to go through the draft for the Vietnam War. For the one and only time I can remember, my father actually initiated a phone call to us, asking Jeff and I to go out to lunch.

During that meal, he told us what war was really like should we have to go. He related a number of stories of his experience as a combat infantryman in the Pacific during World War II, but he emphasized one thing in particular that left a razor's-edge impression.

"The best advice I got when we landed at Guadalcanal came from an old sergeant," he said. "He was a World War I retread, and he was hard as nails. But he told us our first night in the jungle, 'Men, if you want to stay alive, always dig your foxhole two deep.'"

In other words, when the nights are terrifyingly long, and when you have an enemy committed to your destruction, you want a buddy in there with you to fight alongside you.

In many ways, that counsel is at the heart of this second promise. Namely, a man of God is committed to developing vital, growing relationships with other men who can stand alongside him, help guard his back, and even correct him if necessary. We all need men who will consistently exhort and challenge us to be our best, and for whom we can do the same as each of us seeks to stay in the battle and be faithful to his commitments.

Two key aspects of this second promise stand out. The first is something burned into my memory.

A godly man is committed to his brothers.

Back in the summer of 1994, some 50,000 of us stood in the dark in Boulder, Colorado's, Folsom Field, and a single match was lit. That match lit one candle, then that candle lit another, and on and on the flame went until that single spark began to look like a wave of light sweeping the stadium. As we held our candles, prayed, and sang together, suddenly one of the Promise Keepers staff near me began to groan.

It wasn't that he had any lack of awe for what God was doing in each man's life that weekend. It's just that he suddenly realized that a number of men had never gotten those white paper circles— *the ones with holes just the size to fit a candle and catch the hot, dripping wax.*

That was certainly true in the section I was in. And while I didn't see a single man drop his candle, a lot of us were switching hands frequently!

I'm not sure why the wax protectors didn't get to everyone, but I thought it was great! You see, it's easy for some of us to go to a stadium event or other exciting meeting and say, "I'm a promise keeper!" But for those men who had hot wax dripping down their hands, it *cost* them something to keep hold of those candles that signified their desire to live for God.

Genuine commitment is costly. There's no doubt about it. And that's particularly true when we seek to have a relationship with our brothers that's significant and real, not just superficial. It will cost us time, energy, and effort to build and maintain close friendships. But the effort is well worth it. When our foxholes are two (or more) deep, we can keep fighting for God's best in a hostile world.

A godly man pursues vital relationships.

The commitment we make to our brothers is to build vital relationships. The *American Heritage Dictionary* gives this definition for the word *vital:* "Necessary for the continuation of life." That's pretty vital!

In Army Airborne Ranger school, on the first day of training, each man is assigned a "Ranger buddy." Your job—and his—is to see that you each make it through the training alive! Through days of forced marches and grueling physical and tactical training designed to weed out all but the best, your Ranger buddy is to pick you up when you fall down. He's to offer a word of encouragement if he can, or at least a look, when the drill instructor is breathing down your neck. He's to keep pace with you so that you both do more than either of you could have done alone.

The book of Ecclesiastes puts it this way:

> Two are better than one,
>> because they have a good return for their work:
> If one falls down,
>> his friend can help him up.
> But pity the man who falls
>> and has no one to help him up! (4:9-10)

That's the kind of vital relationship with a few brothers in Christ to which we commit ourselves in promise two.

LIVING IT OUT

By his own admission, Kurt Stansell is a sex addict. Kurt is also one of those men most acquaintances look at as someone who "has it all." Married for 13 years to a wonderful wife named Martha, he's the father of an eight-year-old son and a three-year-old daughter. Kurt's also one of the founding elders of his church, which is among the fastest-growing evangelical congregations in the Bay Area of California. His pastors and fellow lay leaders all praise his spiritual leadership. One of them even went so far as to call him "an awesome man of God" who has been and is being used in a mighty way by the Lord.

Kurt Stansell is one of the last people anyone who knew him would have suspected of having a problem with sexual addiction. (We refer to it as an addiction because, as you'll see, it's powerful, it's cyclical in nature, and it leads progressively downward.) But he did. And he does.

"I grew up in a strong Christian home," Kurt says. "My dad was a military chaplain, so we moved a lot, and I spent several years of my youth in Europe and the Far East."

His downfall came with his initial exposure to pornography. "It was a casual, almost accidental thing at first," he says. "I was walking along the streets of Manila when I passed a newsstand overflowing with pornographic magazines. Unlike most displays in the U.S., where only the magazine logo is displayed, everything was out in the open—plastered all over. I didn't stop to look that day. But after that, every time I walked past a newsstand, I'd slow my pace ever so slightly and cast a few furtive glances at the covers of those magazines. Just that bit of exposure proved enough to fuel my adolescent fantasies and more guilt."

By the time Kurt graduated from college, he and Martha were engaged and planned to be married the following year. In the meantime, he took some time off to travel, visiting the missionary family of one of his college roommates in Brazil for several weeks. He concluded his trip with a week alone in Rio de Janeiro.

While there, Kurt discovered an X-rated theater just a couple blocks down from his hotel. "I walked right by it several times in my comings and goings," he says, "and each time the temptation to stop and go in grew a little stronger. Finally, it just seemed too easy to cough up the dollar or so it cost to walk in. I was surprised at how many people were inside. It was fairly full. There were actually couples there on dates.

"Before the movie ended, I slipped out of the theater with a tremendous sense of self-loathing. *You've really hit rock bottom now,* I told myself. *This is the most disgusting thing you've ever done. You can never tell anyone you could have been tempted by, let alone gone in and watched, a movie like that.*"

Kurt went back to his room, got down on his knees, asked God to forgive him, and promised never to do anything like that again. And when he got back to the States and began anticipating his upcoming wedding, he thought, *Marriage will be terrific. That'll be the end of this kind of temptation. I'll have a legitimate sexual release. That'll be the solution.* Unfortunately, it wasn't.

A pattern developed and continued for years. At home in Atlanta, there were periodic stops at convenience-store magazine racks, an occasional X-rated video rental when he knew Martha wasn't going to be home, and excuses made during shopping trips together so he could slip into a bookstore by himself. Visits to live entertainment clubs were reserved for out-of-town business trips.

The Stansells moved to San Jose, California, when Kurt got a big promotion. They soon got into an exciting new church, where Kurt joined a weekly men's prayer breakfast and he and Martha eagerly joined a care group of couples their ages. "I really felt a desperate need for fellowship," Kurt admits. Another guy asked him to team teach a Sunday school class, and Kurt's strong Bible background got him selected to help lead yet another care group. He and a fellow who had been in both groups also agreed to have an accountability relationship, and they began getting together one on one every week.

"I really liked Stan," Kurt says. "He was a terrific Christian guy—someone I thought I could relate to and be honest with. Not that I was very honest with him in the beginning. I'd tell myself, *As soon as I get my act together with this pornography business, I'm going to have 100 percent accountability with Stan. There's no way I can share where I've been; it's just too shameful. He'd never be able to accept me.*"

The two men started meeting for breakfast every week, and Kurt used a lot of euphemisms to avoid getting too specific. "Well, I really screwed up this week. I saw something I shouldn't have," he'd say. "But I think we both knew I was talking about masturbation," he says now.

Despite the limited openness, Kurt's relationship with Stan was positive and encouraging. They challenged each other to be better Christian men, better husbands, and better fathers. Yet the sexual sins continued.

In Kurt's words, "I was like a plane that's gone into a nosedive—heading down, down, down. My meetings with Stan were like when the pilot pulls up on the stick yet feels this tremendous G-force pulling him down harder even after he begins to come out of the dive. The momentum is still there, dragging him down. That's kind of where I was. I was making the right moves with this accountability business, but there was such a momentum in my life—the denial, the impaired thinking, the rationalization. All the patterns of temptation, all the trigger points, were still there."

On his next business trip, after a week alone in Houston, he began to feel the urge. He went to a topless entertainment club and paid one of the women to dance for him. Back in his hotel room later, he thought, *Now you've really hit bottom*. He had never interacted with a person before. "To top it off," he says, "on this same trip to Houston, there had been a very attractive girl in the training class with me. I'd talked to her during breaks, and we had lunch together a couple times. I actually witnessed to her. But by the end of that week, I went home thinking, *You're not invulnerable to an affair. If you'd been in Houston another two weeks, at the rate you were going, you could have really messed up*."

That thought scared him enough that he determined to make his accountability work by being honest with Stan. He still didn't divulge everything, but he told Stan more than he had before. Then Kurt learned that a man who had played a major role in his spiritual development had been accused of sexual misconduct and had seen his ministry come to an end. "That news was the straw that broke the camel's back for me," Kurt says. "That was what said to me, 'Kurt, you are going down in flames unless you can be 100 percent honest.'"

He also thought, *Someday you're going to get caught, and it would be really good if you had at least one person who could testify that you went kicking and screaming, that you were fighting against this addiction.*

One night when their families had gotten together, Kurt and Stan went for a walk. Out on the street, Kurt asked, "Stan, what's the worst thing you've ever done in your whole life?"

Stan described a sexual experience he had years before. "I could see it was hard for him to tell me; it was something that still haunted him," Kurt says. "He worried, 'What if a child was born?' He said he had this recurring nightmare of a kid coming back and saying, 'Hey, Dad.'"

Hearing Stan's story made Kurt want to tell his. But Stan's incident had happened a long time ago, back when he was still a young, single man. Kurt's story was painfully fresh, going on every day even though he was an elder in the church. "I nearly choked on the words," Kurt says, "but I got them out. Stan listened. He didn't condemn me. We prayed for each other."

After praying with Stan, Kurt noticed an immediate difference. "The temptation I faced was cut in half," he explains. "Not that I didn't mess up again. I did. But often when I knew I was going to be on a business trip, or when I felt the temptation building, I'd tell Stan or just think about having to tell him if I gave in, and there truly was less of a temptation.

"As I prayed and as I honestly talked about the issue with Stan," Kurt says, "I began to understand what shame does. When we Christians try to hide something in the darkness, we give Satan incredible license to work in our lives. It's like handing power tools over to him and saying, 'Here, do what you will in my life,' because he's got free rein with all that's hidden when God's light is not shining on it. So I learned that the more open I could be, the less of a hold Satan seemed to have."

Kurt Stansell is quick to admit that the struggle isn't over—the war goes on. But he has found a number of weapons to use in his ongoing battle with temptation. The first is honesty and communication with his wife. He eventually told her about his addiction, and by God's grace they were able to work through their issues and feelings and make their marriage stronger than ever. Now they make honest interaction a high priority, even if some days they can take only five minutes in bed at night to ask, "Where are you tonight? Where are we?"

At the same time, Kurt believes strongly in the need for some other regular accountability—a guy like Stan whom he can go to without burdening Martha with the emotional load of his day-to-day temptations; someone he can call to say, "I'm feeling weak today" or "I feel a strong desire to go look at magazines today."

Last but certainly not least, Kurt is developing a level of trust in God that's deeper than ever. "I've finally learned that God's instructions for us are there for a reason," Kurt says. "He really does want what's best for me; He's not making up the rules arbitrarily. And when we follow His plan and work for His ideal, He amazes us with His blessing and the natural consequences that follow."

YOUR TURN

Having read an overview of promise two and Kurt Stansell's story of trying to live it out, it's your turn to develop an initial plan of your own in this area by completing the forms that follow. Then move them into your daily planner/organizer.

CLOSING THE GAP

A Promise Keeper Is Committed to Pursuing Vital Relationships with Other Men

Personal Evaluation Point

On a scale of 1 to 10, indicate by drawing a line where you stand in reference to promise two. Then fill in the area below the line.

Setting a Prayerful Horizon

Lord willing, 3 years from now my life will reflect this promise in these ways:

My age today _____

3 years from now _____

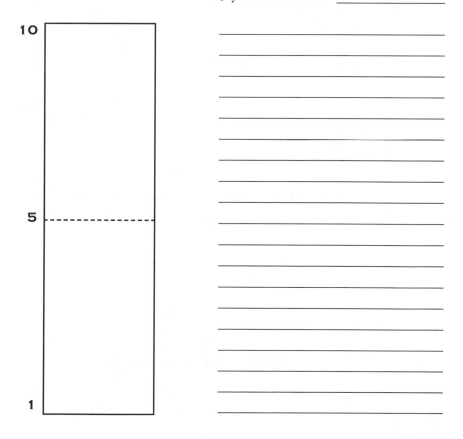

CLOSING THE GAP

2

Action Plan Worksheet

 Knowing that I need to improve in this commitment, I will do my best to take a step of growth by following through in the three areas listed below:

1. *Action Point*

_____

_____

Potential Barrier

_____

_____

2. *Action Point*

_____

_____

Potential Barrier

_____

_____

3. *Action Point*

_____

_____

Potential Barrier

_____

_____

Accountability Commitment

Who _____

When _____

Now move your plan into the appropriate places in your daily planner.

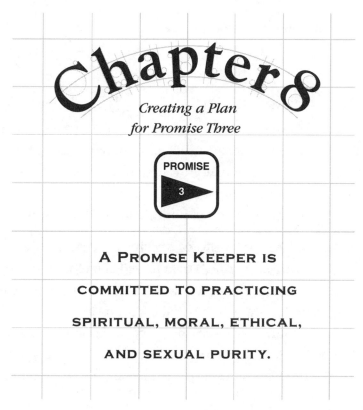

Chapter 8

Creating a Plan
for Promise Three

PROMISE
3

A PROMISE KEEPER IS COMMITTED TO PRACTICING SPIRITUAL, MORAL, ETHICAL, AND SEXUAL PURITY.

Core issue: faithfulness
Key passage to review in your group: 1 Corinthians 4:2

Picture being out on a hike in the woods with your children. They're young and thrilled to be in the "great outdoors" with their dad. Yet with their little legs, they struggle to keep up with you. And after going all of 100 yards, they tire and ask the inevitable "hiking" question:

"Daddy, can we have a drink of water, please?"

"Sure, kids," you say.

You proceed to open a canteen of water and fill a cup for your beloved children. Only the water is brown, not crystal clear. In fact, you realize it's filthy, polluted water, laced with contaminants.

Would you give a thirsty child you love a drink of such water? Of course not.

How tragic it is, however, when little ones look up at their father and soak in the impurities of his godless lifestyle! Have no doubt: Children will soak in your level of anger, lust, deception, or corruption like a sponge. But it doesn't have to be that way if you commit yourself to the third promise of a godly man, which is to maintain a life of moral, ethical, spiritual, and sexual purity. Then they'll be getting "fresh water" every day.

Let's look at each of those aspects of purity, beginning with spiritual purity.

A godly man seeks to live a life of spiritual purity.

"Create in me a pure heart, O God," David prayed in Psalm 51:10. David, we're told in Scripture, was a man after God's own heart. Yet even great saints—when they walk away from God's Word—can commit great sins.

At the time David penned the words to that powerful song, he had fallen into terrible sin. He had initiated an affair with a beautiful married woman named Bathsheba, and then he had cunningly plotted the murder of her husband, Uriah the Hittite.

We pay a price when we fail to remain pure in our thoughts and actions. In a sister psalm, David wrote, "When I kept silent [about my sin], my bones wasted away through my groaning all day long. For day and night your hand was heavy upon me; my strength was sapped as in the heat of summer" (Psalm 32:3-4).

Is there any antidote to the catastrophic cost of leading an impure life?

David continued, "I said, 'I will confess my transgressions to the LORD'—and you forgave the guilt of my sin" (verse 5).

Spiritual purity involves confessing our sins, for "if we confess our sins, he is faithful and just and will forgive us our sins and purify us from all unrighteousness" (1 John 1:9). It also involves doing what's right, not continuing to sin just because God forgives us, so that "grace may increase" (Romans 6:1).

A godly man seeks to live a life of ethical purity.

Bob was the fourth Scout leader one group of boys had had in a single year. Through a series of unrelated incidents, each of the other leaders had left quickly. It seems that Bob was now the only one willing to volunteer.

Bob had been a Scout himself as a boy, but his had been an inactive troop. So he decided the first night he stood before these young men that he'd do things differently in his own troop. "We're not just going to sit around on Scout night," he confidently promised. "We're going to prepare for and go on a camping trip!"

He thought there would be a yell of support and delight.

What he got were bored stares and rude snickers.

Later he learned why. On the way out of the meeting that night, he stopped one of the boys and asked why they didn't want to go camping. "We want to go camping," the boy told him. "But the last three Scout leaders all said the same thing you did their first night. And we still haven't gone camping."

Could those to whom we make promises make the same kind of accusation against us? Or are we men like Bob—who followed through on his promise to those boys with a camping trip. In fact, they traveled more than 1,000 miles to camp at the bottom of the Grand Canyon!

If we're to live with ethical purity, we're committed to following through on our promises. Even more, *ethical purity* involves steering clear of anything that might sully our name or bring reproach on the Savior. That includes shady business deals, controversial linkages that might "blow up" if exposed, or even associating with shady characters. As God's Word says, "Do not be misled: 'Bad company corrupts good character'" (1 Corinthians 15:33).

A godly man seeks to live a life of moral and sexual purity.

There's no secret or surprise here. Paul told us in no uncertain words, "Do you not know that your bodies are members of Christ himself? Shall I then take the members of Christ and unite them with a prostitute? Never!" (1 Corinthians 6:15).

Let's face it, sexual sin is exciting, titillating, alluring. But as the book of Proverbs tells us, we pay an incredible price when we cave in to that excitement and fail to see the terrible hook behind it.

> All at once he followed her
> like an ox going to the slaughter,

> like a deer stepping into a noose
>> till an arrow pierces his liver,
> like a bird darting into a snare,
>> little knowing it will cost him his life. (7:22-23)

That's serious stuff. And it's also why the Scriptures are so serious about the need to "flee from sexual immorality" (1 Corinthians 6:18), to not allow it a place in our lives. Joseph set the example when he ran from Potiphar's wife. Paul reaffirmed the thought there in 1 Corinthians 6. It takes only a few drops of ink to color a glass of water. We can't traffic in even small amounts of pornography, coarse talk, or flirting if we're serious about living in moral and sexual purity.

To pull off this part of promise three takes the gut-level honesty and spiritual strength to walk away from temptation, not make small talk with it. Don't think you're strong enough to turn back before it's too late; you'll lose if you do.

It helps if, by the time you tackle this promise, you've already nailed down promises one and two. If your commitment to Christ is solid, as is your commitment to a small group of brothers, you've got two strong supports already. The Holy Spirit, along with those brothers in Christ, can ask you the hard questions of accountability and encourage you to live in purity.

The good news is that if we're faithful to keep this promise, we hand our children a glass filled with sweet, cool, crystal clear water.

LIVING IT OUT

Suppose you're in charge of the biggest project in your company's history, and due to factors beyond your control, things aren't going as well as everyone would like. To obscure that fact, you're asked to play accounting games. Failure to do so might cost your company the contract and could cost you your job. What course would you choose?

That's the kind of dilemma Jeff Vaughn faced a few years ago. After attending a weekend conference in 1993, he told Promise Keepers about the struggle he had encountered in applying his faith to his responsibilities at a leading aero-space company.

At Jeff's work, every program handled by his company is assigned a management team whose job it is to oversee the fulfillment of the contract. Jeff, as one of those executives, is responsible for cost and schedule management. "In other words," he explains, "it's my job to make sure my company delivers whatever piece of hardware or software we're developing to our client on schedule and for the price specified in our contract."

Part of the challenge of managing such long-term, multimillion-dollar contracts is keeping up with the constant changes in specifications and plans being made by the client's engineers or at the whim of politicians who ultimately control the purse strings of any government project. This liaison role requires extensive interaction with the client's representatives through management reviews, progress reports, briefings, and on-site inspections.

Jeff began work on a space-station program that was the most challenging and troublesome project he and his company had ever tackled. The sheer size of the overall program and the multitude of subcontractors involved made logistics difficult enough. To complicate things even further, constant engineering changes by NASA and higher-level contractors resulted in literally hundreds of contract changes for Jeff's company. And Jeff, whose job it was to monitor every change so costs and schedule could be adjusted accordingly, was sometimes months and hundreds of contract changes behind because his company's client wasn't communicating those changes in a timely manner.

"It was a logistical and managerial nightmare," he says.

What routinely happens in such programs is that contractors seldom acknowledge cost overruns during the early years. Instead, for example, a contractor given an annual budget of $100 million to provide this and that will issue reports indicating it did, indeed, spend no more than the budgeted $100 million to provide this and some of that—with the rest of "that" now scheduled to come out of next year's $100 million budget. But then, unless costs can be cut somewhere else (which is very unlikely), a snowball effect kicks in, and something else has to be pushed to the following year to allow for the conclusion of the previous year's goals. If that pattern continues, the hidden problem gets bigger and bigger until the truth finally comes out. And by then, everyone usually has too much invested to abandon the project, so all that can be done is to appropriate additional funds for the remaining years of the program or extend the project a few years (which amounts to the same thing).

This is just what happened with NASA's massive space-station program. "Every year I was on the program, we fought a constant battle, because of the continuous changes, to live within the funding for the year and to deliver what we'd promised on schedule," Jeff says. "The pressure came right down the line from NASA to our client and all the other contractors. If everyone didn't deliver everything we were supposed to deliver at the cost we had contracted for, not only would we look bad, but our client and its client would look bad all the way up to NASA. And then, when Congress scrutinized NASA's budget, if the program looked as though it had serious overrun problems, the politicians might well terminate the entire project. That would mean not only billions of dollars a year to corporate America, but also thousands of jobs in our company and throughout the entire aerospace industry."

Jeff admits, "I lost a lot of sleep trying to figure out how our company was going to do what we'd contracted to do."

Jeff eventually concluded it simply couldn't be done—that there were going to be cost overruns. Then he wrestled with just what to tell his superiors, because he knew they wouldn't like the unvarnished truth. Ultimately, however, as a Christian and a man of integrity, Jeff decided that was the only way to go. But when he turned in his conclusions, he received intense pressure to manipulate his figures.

One of his bosses called Jeff into his office and said, "You can't tell me that you can sit here and know for a fact that we can't make up enough ground in the remaining years of this program to meet our delivery schedule. Surely you have to admit there's a chance we can deliver on time."

Jeff admitted he couldn't say with certainty what would happen five years down the road. "But the possibility is very, very slim," he maintained. "And based on my evaluation, I feel there is no way we can fulfill the contract."

Despite that kind of pressure from within his own company, Jeff felt he had no choice but to be just as honest with his company's client—who was no more eager than his bosses to face the truth. After Jeff and the rest of his team presented the numbers and got a cold reception, they retreated to a conference room to rehash their projections. In time, they all agreed there was no way to do the contracted work for less money. So when the team leader argued for the usual postpone-some-of-the-work-to-a-later-date trick, the team finally agreed—but only after Jeff and others who backed him insisted on being completely open with the client. They would agree to the original amount of funding budgeted as long as they spelled out in careful, written detail what parts of the contract could not be fulfilled or would have to be delayed until the following fiscal year.

As a man of integrity, Jeff says, "I had an obligation to my company and our client to make sure they clearly understood my position—that we could no longer expect to do what we'd promised on the schedule or at the cost we'd agreed to when we signed the original contract. I had to do what I thought was right. And it was up to my superiors, our client, and ultimately their clients to decide what to do with the information I provided."

Someone somewhere made the decision to continue hiding the truth about cost overruns. But the whole thing blew wide open the following year, and Congress held hearings, calling in NASA officials and executives from numerous contractors and subcontractors. As a result, the entire space-station program was scaled back and restructured to include a new partnership with the Russians. In the process, several companies, including Jeff's, lost huge contracts. Many jobs were lost, including those of some of Jeff's superiors. But he was transferred to another team overseeing the cost and scheduling management of one of his company's contracts with the Pentagon.

Jeff will never know for sure, but his carefully documented insistence on honestly reporting his company's part of the space-station program may be one reason he's closing in on a 25-year pin while so many in his industry are out of work. "God has been good," he says. "And I now sleep better than ever."

YOUR TURN

Having read an overview of promise three and Jeff Vaughn's story of trying to live it out, it's your turn to develop an initial plan of your own in this area by completing the forms that follow. Then move your plan into your daily planner/organizer.

CLOSING THE GAP

A Promise Keeper Is Committed to Practicing Integrity

Personal Evaluation Point

On a scale of 1 to 10, indicate by drawing a line where you stand in reference to promise three. Then fill in the area below the line.

Setting a Prayerful Horizon

Lord willing, 3 years from now my life will reflect this promise in these ways:

My age today   _____
3 years from now   _____

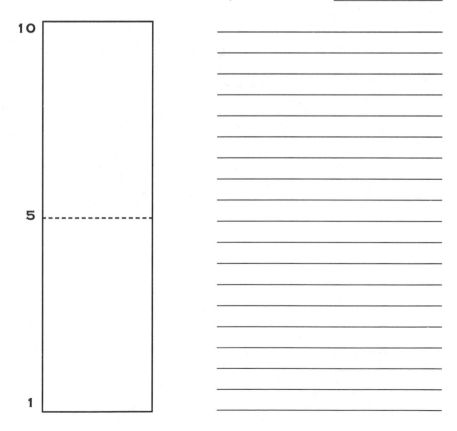

CLOSING THE GAP

3

Action Plan Worksheet

 Knowing that I need to improve in this commitment, I will do my best to take a step of growth by following through in the three areas listed below:

1. *Action Point*

_____

_____

Potential Barrier

_____

_____

2. *Action Point*

_____

_____

Potential Barrier

_____

_____

3. *Action Point*

_____

_____

Potential Barrier

_____

_____

Accountability Commitment

Who _____

When _____

Now move your plan into the appropriate places in your daily planner.

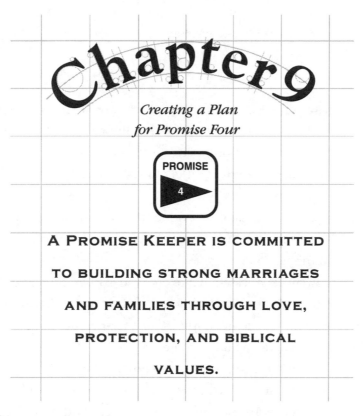

Chapter 9

Creating a Plan
for Promise Four

PROMISE 4

A Promise Keeper is committed to building strong marriages and families through love, protection, and biblical values.

 Core issue: servanthood
Key passage to review in your group: Matthew 20:27

Whether we're single or married, we're told in God's Word that we're to provide for our families. That doesn't mean we have to provide our mother with a pink Cadillac or our spouse with a three-story house. But it does mean that in those areas that are most important, we take our family relationships seriously, particularly as we reflect the following three biblical traits.

A godly man serves his family.

Think just a moment about what a faithful butler is like, perhaps in an old movie you have seen. Got a picture in mind? What made that person so treasured in the home? He was an outstanding servant. He anticipated the master's needs. He did things that promoted the best interests of those in the family, and he protected them if necessary.

Men, servant leadership is a clear calling in Scripture. We're expressly told not to "lord it over" anyone as the kings of the Gentiles did—including our wives (see Luke 22:25-26). Rather, Scripture gives us guidelines on the type of sacrificial love it takes to make a marriage reflect Christ's love.

For example, consider the way one woman in the Bible drew a picture of a loving servant leader, her husband. "Draw me after you and let us run together!" Solomon's bride told him (Song of Solomon 1:4, NASB). Notice how much firepower there is in this verse.

Without a doubt, she was asking him to take the lead in the home. "Draw me after you," she said, not "Follow me." But once he took the lead, there was mutuality and sharing. There was no inferiority of one person compared to the other, yet there was clear leadership and structure.

Did you know the only other time the word *draw* is used in Scripture, it's used of God, "drawing us" to Himself with His love? For example, God told Hosea, "I led [literally, *drew*] them with cords of human kindness, with ties of love; I lifted the yoke from their neck and bent down to feed them" (Hosea 11:4).

Moses used the same language to praise the Lord: "During the forty years that I led [literally, *drew*] you through the desert, your clothes did not wear out, nor did the sandals on your feet" (Deuteronomy 29:5).

And in Jeremiah 31:3, God spoke to His people and said, "I have loved you with an everlasting love; I have drawn you with loving-kindness."

Put all three of those verses together and you've got a powerful picture of a servant leader.

A servant leader is someone who takes the lead in loving his wife. He leads in serving her. And he leads in sensitivity, compassion, and caring for her needs.

Do you think living out these three aspects of leadership with your wife would bring her closer to you or drive her away?

Servant leadership isn't resented by a wife, because it reflects a husband who is seeking to love his wife as Christ loved the church. ("Husbands, love your wives, just as Christ loved the church and gave himself up for her" [Ephesians

5:25].) It means proactively meeting her needs, listening instead of lecturing, praising and building up instead of tearing down. This isn't abdicating our position of leadership but following the example of our Lord.

A godly man protects his family.

Is it safe to live in your home?

I don't mean, do you live in a gated suburban community or have a state-of-the-art alarm system? I mean, is your home a safe place for the people who live with you? Is it safe for them to express their thoughts, dreams, failures, and fears? Is it safe enough for them to ask questions without your criticizing, or for them to have a "bad day" without fearing you'll withdraw and cut them off emotionally for days to come?

Physical protection is just one of the ways we're to safeguard our loved ones. Without a doubt, the most important protection we can offer our wives and children is in our prayers. That may sound like something right out of a sermon, but it's true. In fact, even surveys illustrate the power of prayer.

For example, statistics reveal that the divorce rate in the United States is roughly one in two—that is, one marriage out of every two will end in divorce. Tragically, the Gallup Poll shows that the divorce rate for people who say they are evangelical Christians is no different from that of the general population. *But note one powerful difference that surfaced in the Gallup organization's extensive research of believers:* For those couples who pray together every night, the divorce rate goes from one in two to—hold on to your hat—*1 in 1,052.* (See Commissioned Research on "Evangelical Christians," Gallup Research Corporation summary report, May 1991.)

I mention this not because God's Word needs any independent verification, but because it amazes me how science always eventually catches up to the Scriptures.

The way the Lord Jesus prayed for protection for His followers gives us a model of how we can put up a spiritual hedge around ourselves and our families. As with Job, God may still allow us to encounter times of severe testing. But He remains faithful to us and our families when we are committed prayer warriors.

A godly man teaches biblical values in his home.

"Train a child in the way he should go, and when he is old he will not turn from it," we're told in the familiar proverb (22:6). And it's true! Teaching biblical truths is a powerful way of instilling godly values that can provide a secure foundation for later growth.

In Old Testament times, Scripture verses were written over the doorways of a home, on bracelets, and on headbands. These prominently displayed verses were a testimony to all who entered or saw the people that "as for me and my household, we will serve the LORD" (Joshua 24:15).

If we're to give our children such training, we need to take spiritual disciplines seriously ourselves and not push quiet times on our kids when we never open the Bible ourselves. And it means we search for those "teachable moments"—driving in the car or playing in the backyard—when we can discuss a verse, raise a question that makes them think, or challenge them to live for Christ.

Through being a servant, providing protection, upholding our families in prayer, and consistently teaching biblical values, we can go a long way toward keeping this vitally important promise.

LIVING IT OUT

As the parents of two adopted children, Joel and Lena Treadaway never imagined the ordeal ahead of them. It began when the adoption agency that had placed Danny and Sara called to tell them about an unwanted newborn boy with a terminal heart problem in a nearby hospital. The baby had suffered one massive heart attack right after birth. The next would almost certainly kill him. Doctors expected him to die at any moment. But in the meantime, the agency was looking for a couple who knew something about neonatal heart problems and would be willing to visit and hold and comfort the little boy.

One visit to the hospital nursery was enough to convince both Joel and Lena that they wanted to adopt Seth. Within three weeks, the little guy amazed the doctors by growing strong enough for the Treadaways to take him home. But two days later, his heart stopped, and he had to be resuscitated and rushed back into the hospital. The doctors gave him six months to live—maximum.

Countless people prayed for Seth. As he grew bigger and stronger, his astonished doctors considered him a miracle boy. His heart stopped on several occasions, but each time the Treadaways or some medical personnel were able to revive him. He was in and out of the hospital for months. And when he was home, he required 24-hour-a-day attention.

Joel bonded with Seth in a way that amazed Lena and gave her a new depth of love and admiration for her husband. But Joel's devotion to Seth also gave her reason to worry: The longer their son defied medical odds, the more Joel wanted to believe that Seth might actually be able to live a normal life someday.

About the time Seth turned four, Lena began to sense a subtle but steady decline in his overall strength, yet Joel couldn't (or wouldn't) see it. But then maybe he subconsciously saw what was coming, because he began to withdraw from the family by becoming more and more wrapped up in his work.

One afternoon a few weeks later, while sitting peacefully in Lena's lap, Seth stopped breathing. As she laid him quickly on his bed and began administering CPR, she yelled for Danny to call 911 and then Joel's office. But she knew her son was gone.

Despite finding some initial comfort from the beauty and meaningfulness of the funeral service, the Treadaways were only beginning the grief process. "I went very quickly from denial, to sorrow, to anger," Joel acknowledges. From there, unable to process his own feelings, let alone anyone else's, he withdrew from the family and began burying himself in his work. A trial lawyer, he accepted a number of out-of-town cases. One took him away from home for three weeks, another for 10 days.

"Suddenly I needed him, and he was never there," Lena says.

Joel says now, "It pains me to admit it, but I just quit nurturing my wife. I couldn't worry about her or my other children. It was selfishness on my part, but my number-one priority became me."

Mostly, however, Joel was mad at God. He had a long list of questions he wanted God to answer: Why did You have to take Seth now? Were You just trifling with us by keeping him alive so long? Were we just too happy? Didn't You think we'd had enough pain? Didn't we do enough to justify having Seth? Did You expect us to pray harder or have more faith? Hearing no answers made Joel even angrier.

While Joel continued to pour his primary energies into his work, he knew he had to do something to help Lena and his children cope. So they scheduled a number of family trips in that first year after Seth's death, including one to the Grand Canyon to begin the summer of 1993.

The trouble was that Joel couldn't hide in his work on vacation, so his emotional withdrawal seemed even more painfully obvious. "On one level, the spectacular beauty of the Grand Canyon was a great distraction," he says. "We did a lot of hiking and other memorable activities with Danny and Sara. But I don't know that I said 10 words to Lena the whole trip. That wasn't like me, at least not the old me. We all felt the tension. And it scared me. Somewhere I'd read that the great majority of couples who experience the loss of a child end up getting a divorce. I didn't want to be a part of those statistics."

A friend invited Joel to Promise Keepers in Boulder. He declined, saying he had a trial starting that week. But when the case settled at the last minute, Joel called his friend back and said he'd go after all. He was desperate for answers; maybe he'd find some there.

When Joel got to Boulder, he heard Dr. James Dobson speak on "What Your Wife Wants Me to Tell You." Joel says, "It was as if he sat right down beside me and started pointing out what God, my friend Mike, and Lena had been trying to tell me all along and I just hadn't been hearing. He talked about how a man who wants to be happy and healthy and everything God wants him to be needs to be making his wife and his wife's needs a priority. How God honors that. How we need to be careful to make sure our priorities reflect God's priorities for our lives."

The more Dobson talked, the bigger failure Joel realized he'd been. When his wife and family needed him most, he simply hadn't been there for them. By the time Dobson finished, Joel was nearly overcome by guilt and remorse. He asked God to forgive him and help him get his life back in balance. And he vowed to do whatever it took to prove to his wife and children how important they were.

Joel flew home to Miami on Sunday morning. From the airport, he hurried right to church. "The moment I spotted Lena after the service, I grabbed hold of her and kissed her for what seemed like 15 minutes!" he says. "I just couldn't turn her loose. I guess she knew right then that something had happened!"

For nearly a year, Joel's withdrawal had kept Lena and their children from dealing with their own grief and questions regarding Seth's death. He now realized how much they all still had to work through. He encouraged her to dump on him all the pain she'd bottled up for so long. He talked openly with Danny and Sara about their feelings and his. Together as a family, they would sometimes discuss their good memories of Seth.

As he reinvested himself in the everyday routine of his family and reestablished a healthy balance in his priorities, Joel began to get a perspective he hadn't had when everything got so out of whack. "As I focused on making my family a priority again," he says, "as I tried to fulfill Lena's and Danny's and Sara's needs, it began to dawn on me that Seth doesn't need me now, because he's in heaven. He's already enjoying what the rest of us will have to wait for. He's not sick anymore; he's just fine.

"It was Danny and Sara who needed me now. I was the only dad they had. They were entitled to my love, attention, and time. I was the only husband Lena had. She, too, needed to know she was a priority. And I'd have to work at making sure that happened."

The Treadaways both acknowledge that keeping their priorities in healthy balance takes determination and planning. Every couple of weeks, Joel and Lena sit down with his work calendar and their family calendar to schedule upcoming events and responsibilities and resolve potential conflicts as far in advance as possible.

Joel also recommends looking for ways to squeeze quality time out of ordinary family routines. He cites grocery shopping as an example. He does the family food purchasing every Saturday morning and says Danny and Sara always fight over whose turn it is to go with him. "It's amazing the kinds of things we've talked about while grocery shopping," Joel says.

Joel also puts a renewed emphasis on communication. "Some people may think it's strange," Lena says, "but we do a lot of our talking on the phone. Some days he's gone from home a lot of hours; so when he's home, we want him to spend as much time as he can with the kids. He's a morning person and I'm a night owl, so that adds to the challenge of finding time alone. That's why we end up talking on the phone once or twice every single day—whether he's in town or out."

Furthermore, Joel and Lena say they regularly pray as a family, as a couple, and as individuals. The result is a strong sense of feeling supported, of being important to each other.

Making family a priority sometimes requires compromises or sacrifices in other areas of life, as Joel has discovered. For example, he consistently turns down opportunities and responsibilities within his own law firm. He begs off internal committee assignments, explaining that with the demands of his practice and his family, his plate is more than full. "Our compensation is determined in part by the extent of our involvement in firm activities," he says. "So my not being so involved does cost me money." But evidently enough of Joel's colleagues respect his priorities that he continues to succeed professionally and as a partner in the firm.

For Joel, his re-establishment of priorities has certainly been worth it. After 20 years of marriage, he says, "Lena and I have a great relationship again. She's my best friend. If there's anyone in the world I wish I could spend more time with, it's her."

Lena adds, "For a time there, I thought our marriage was over. It may as well have been. But I have my husband back now. He's alive again. There's an intensity of love I haven't felt since our newlywed days. For a long time after Joel came home from Boulder, I kept waiting for his mountaintop glow to fade. But that glow has remained steady ever since. The balance we have yearned for is here. We can almost touch the peace."

YOUR TURN

Having read an overview of promise four and Joel Treadaway's story of trying to live it out, it's your turn to develop an initial plan of your own in this area by completing the forms that follow. Then transfer your plan to your daily planner/organizer.

CLOSING THE GAP

A Promise Keeper Is Committed to Building a Strong Marriage and Family

Personal Evaluation Point

On a scale of 1 to 10, indicate by drawing a line where you stand in reference to promise four. Then fill in the area below the line.

Setting a Prayerful Horizon

Lord willing, 3 years from now my life will reflect this promise in these ways:

My age today _____

3 years from now _____

_____
_____
_____
_____
_____
_____
_____
_____
_____
_____
_____
_____
_____
_____
_____
_____
_____
_____
_____

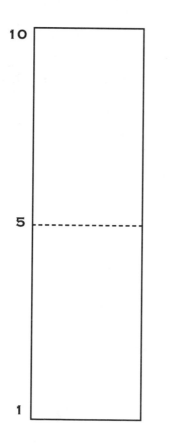

CLOSING THE GAP

Action Plan Worksheet

Knowing that I need to improve in this commitment, I will do my best to take a step of growth by following through in the three areas listed below:

1. *Action Point*

_____

_____

Potential Barrier

_____

_____

2. *Action Point*

_____

_____

Potential Barrier

_____

_____

3. *Action Point*

_____

_____

Potential Barrier

_____

_____

Accountability Commitment

Who _____

When _____

Now move your plan into the appropriate places in your daily planner.

Chapter 10

*Creating a Plan
for Promise Five*

PROMISE 5

A PROMISE KEEPER IS COMMITTED TO SUPPORTING THE MISSION OF THE CHURCH BY HONORING AND PRAYING FOR HIS PASTOR, AND BY ACTIVELY GIVING HIS TIME AND RESOURCES.

Core issue: honor

Key passages to review in your group: 1 Thessalonians 5:12-13; Hebrews 13:17

A recent survey of life's "most stressful professions" looked not just at the jobs, but also at which professions placed the most stress on a *spouse.* Guess what came out right at the top? If you guessed the pastorate, you're right.

When you think about those in full-time ministry today, you're looking at people, along with their families, who are on the firing line. From high expectations to long hours to constant financial concerns, the ministry provides a significant challenge—topped off by the spiritual stress of leading a church. But what might surprise you is the *loneliness* that many pastors feel.

It may seem impossible that someone who is constantly with people could feel lonely and overwhelmed. But at times, every pastor, from

Moses on, has felt the crushing burden of leading and teaching God's people.

In Moses' time, his father-in-law, Jethro, came alongside him, gave him wise counsel, and helped him shoulder and spread out some of the load (see Exodus 18). In our day, it's not enough to think "somebody else" is taking care of your pastor. Far too often, everyone thinks, *Oh, he's so busy, I'm not going to bother him,* and then no one calls!

Pastoral burnout is at an all-time high, and one major reason is that our ministers feel no support from their flock. Who helps the helper? That's what this fifth promise of a godly man is about. It's a commitment to not just be a spectator at your church, but to be an active churchman—a genuine friend and consistent support to your pastor and in the mission of the church.

A godly man gives honor to his pastor.

The word *honor* in the Scriptures literally means "to be heavy or weighty." Gold, for example, is heavy and highly valuable. On the other hand, honor's opposite, *dishonor,* literally means "mist or steam."

Can you see the difference in these two pictures and in the application of giving honor to your pastor? When you honor your pastor, you treat him like a "heavyweight." He's worthy of your time and attention, of taking his teaching seriously, and of your personal encouragement and help as God allows.

During the early years of Promise Keepers, one of the most meaningful things that happened at stadium events occurred when all the pastors were called down front on Saturday night. Then the men in the stands cheered and cheered in honor of the pastors' service for the Lord. As I travel the country, I've spoken with more than a dozen pastors who have described that event as one of the most meaningful experiences in their entire ministries—not because they were looking for glory, but because a group of men took the time to thank God for them. And believe me, those stadiums roared!

Perhaps you can't get up and lead cheers for your pastor at a Sunday service, but you can do the two important things found on the next couple of pages.

A godly man supports the mission of the church.

Today, we have so many demands on our time that active involvement in our church can seem like a pressure, not a privilege. That's why many pastors feel they're leading a charge up the hill—only to find when they reach the top that they're alone!

One of the most constructive things you can do is to spend time with your pastor. Take him out to lunch, not with an agenda but simply to ask what his dreams and goals are for the church. Ask what you can pray about for him. Ask about his family, too, and whether there's anything you could do for them. Let him know you value his leadership, you want to be an encouragement to him, and you'll be someone he can count on.

It may take you a week or two to get an appointment. Don't let that put you off. Many men think their pastor works only on Sunday morning. Actually, he never gets to leave the job because it's a calling—a job with no time clock.

With the press of premarital counseling, marriage counseling, sermon preparation, board meetings, staff planning, hospital or home-bound visits, funerals, and more, he's juggling 30 balls at once, just like you. And remember, if he keeps all those balls in the air, he rarely hears any praise. But drop a single ball, and watch out!

One layman who lives in a large city with a major sports team came up with a creative way to encourage his pastor. When he went to lunch with his pastor, it became apparent that the pastor was feeling guilty about having to spend so much time on church business when he had three growing boys at home.

After the luncheon, without telling the pastor, the layman consulted with the chairman of the deacon board and then recruited a dozen men from his church. Next he called the pastor's wife to get her input and tip her off on what he was planning. Together, those 13 men bought two upper-deck season tickets to the team's games and presented them to the pastor. There was just one string attached to the gift: The pastor had to use the tickets to take one of his three boys with him to each of the games!

That pastor told me, almost in tears, what an incredible bonding experience that proved to be for him and his boys. He'd been offered tickets to attend a game with someone in the church several times before, but he'd always turned them down. Why? Because it meant taking more time away from the family. *Now he could go see a game he loved with one of his sons whom he loved much more.*

I'm not saying you have to provide season tickets for your pastor (though tickets to just one game for him and his family would be a great idea). But what those men did was to look at a need their pastor had (to spend time with his sons) and provide a creative way to meet it. And everyone felt encouraged with the result.

A godly man provides resources to the church.

Whenever you say people should "support" their church, they instantly think, *Here we go again—another call for money.* But every church needs adequate resources so the building can be lighted and heated and the pastor can be free from financial pressure and focus on teaching, preaching, and ministering. However, in addition to financial gifts, there are many other ways you can provide resources to your church.

For example, you may have access to some building materials that would save money on an addition the church is building to the youth room. You might volunteer on a work day and provide a strong back to clean or set up the sanctuary. Or you may serve on a board, council, or advisory group, offering anything from sermon research to computer networking.

In our "spectator" culture, people drive by auto accidents without blinking an eye. Don't speed by your pastor, however, only to learn when he burns out (or worse) that he was lonely and hurting. As with all the other six promises, this one involves a cost. But it's a clear mark of a man of God.

LIVING IT OUT

Ralph Heiss pastors an integrated church with attendance running around 150. Soon after Ralph began this church, a number of area pastors from various denominations reached out to invite him to join a fellowship of the city's evangelical clergy. They met every month to encourage one another and occasionally worked together in cooperative efforts like a local crusade. But Ralph routinely turned down all such invitations because, he says, "they weren't believers of my stripe. I'd make excuses, but what I really wanted to say to them was 'Just leave me alone.'"

When the subject of this evangelical pastors' group came up, one of Ralph's denominational colleagues said, "I don't even want to meet them, because I might like them. Then I might have to make some decisions I don't want to make."

It was indirectly because of his denomination's attitude toward other Christian groups that Ralph first heard about Promise Keepers. Bernie, an active member of a nearby congregation of Ralph's denomination, learned about the Colorado conference and decided he wanted to recruit other members of his church to go with him. But Bernie's pastor told him, "It's not our denomination. We're not interested."

Bernie went anyway. And when he returned, he couldn't say enough about the experience. His pastor told him he didn't want to hear anything about it, and because of Bernie's "disobedience" in going, he actually stripped him of his leadership roles in the church and suggested he move his membership to another congregation. The pastor recommended Ralph's church but then called to warn Ralph against giving Bernie any leadership responsibilities.

Ralph was so impressed with Bernie's spiritual commitment, however, that he soon disregarded his fellow pastor's advice. And when Bernie wanted to go hear a singer/evangelist he'd heard about through Promise Keepers, Ralph went with him.

As Ralph tells it, "This musician had played in the NFL, and he was a really dynamic preacher and singer, an awesome black brother. I was so impressed that I helped get him into the public schools to give drug talks to the students. We talked quite a bit, and he challenged me. He said, 'Pastor Heiss, I believe if you'll take 10 men from your congregation to Promise Keepers, your church will never be the same.'"

So Ralph and 12 men from his church signed up to go to the Indianapolis conference in June 1994.

Bernie had told him what to expect. So Ralph went to the conference antici-pating a terrific lineup of speakers who would have a powerful impact on the dozen men in his church. What he never expected was the impact the experi-ence would have on *him*.

It started during a song. Sixty thousand men in the Hoosier Dome stood and sang "Holy, Holy, Holy." "There were all kinds of guys," Ralph says, "from so many different church backgrounds, with all sorts of expressions—some with their hands raised and looking toward heaven, others with their eyes closed and their heads bowed. And it hit me, *Each one of us in his own way is lifting his heart to God. We're not doing anything sinful here. We're doing something wonder-ful and beautiful.*"

Later, at mealtime, those 60,000 men emptied out of the Hoosier Dome onto the streets of downtown Indianapolis. The massive lunch line packed the tunnel where the street passes under the train tracks running into Union Station next door. Somewhere in that huge, surging sea of humanity, somebody started to sing. Within moments, there was a spontaneous song service, with thousands of male voices echoing through the tunnel.

"It was truly one of the most beautiful things I have ever seen or heard," recalls Ralph. "And I couldn't help thinking, *This is just what heaven's going to be like. There's going to be a whole bunch of people who never knew each other, who have different doctrines and different skin colors and different preferences— all just focused on Jesus.*"

Ralph was also impressed by the fact that in that huge, hungry crowd of strangers, he saw no pushing, no shoving, nobody getting impatient, everybody excited, but everyone being gracious.

"Then there was a handful of protesters outside with signs saying 'Jesus is not God' and all sorts of anti-Christian slogans," he says. "I particularly remember one guy wearing a pin that said 'Ex-fundamentalist inside.' I suspect if the tables had been turned, if 60,000 atheists had come out of the Hoosier Dome to find eight or 10 protesters, some people would have died that day. Instead the Promise

Keepers crowd handed these protesters tracts, told them they loved them, invited them inside, and sang to them. And I think that just blew the protesters away. They evidently couldn't deal with it, because the next thing I knew, they had just sort of melted away and were gone."

When the conference started again, Ralph suddenly realized he had been wrong in the way he was treating other Christians. "And I knew without a doubt," he says, "that the first thing I needed to do when I got home was to go to that group of evangelical pastors I'd snubbed for 15 years and apologize for my intolerant attitude."

Thanks to an active, supportive layman named Bernie, Ralph Heiss began to live out biblical reconciliation with his brothers in Christian ministry. Bernie took the time and effort to reach out to his new pastor, and their entire city grew spiritually more healthy as a result.

YOUR TURN

Having read an overview of promise five and Bernie's story of trying to live it out, it's your turn to develop an initial plan of your own in this area by completing the forms that follow. Then transfer your plan to your daily planner/organizer.

CLOSING THE GAP

$$\boxed{5}$$

A Promise Keeper Is Committed to Supporting the Mission of the Church

Personal Evaluation Point

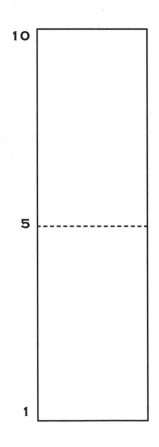 On a scale of 1 to 10, indicate by drawing a line where you stand in reference to promise five. Then fill in the area below the line.

Setting a Prayerful Horizon

Lord willing, 3 years from now my life will reflect this promise in these ways:

My age today _____
3 years from now _____

_____
_____
_____
_____
_____
_____
_____
_____
_____
_____
_____
_____
_____
_____
_____
_____
_____
_____
_____

CLOSING THE GAP

5

Action Plan Worksheet

Knowing that I need to improve in this commitment, I will do my best to take a step of growth by following through in the three areas listed below:

1. *Action Point*

_____

_____

Potential Barrier

_____

_____

2. *Action Point*

_____

_____

Potential Barrier

_____

_____

3. *Action Point*

_____

_____

Potential Barrier

_____

_____

Accountability Commitment

Who _____

When _____

Now move your plan into the appropriate places in your daily planner.

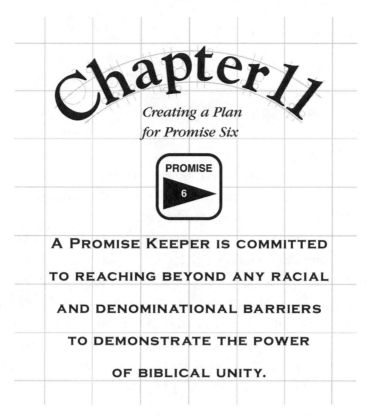

Chapter 11

Creating a Plan
for Promise Six

PROMISE 6

A PROMISE KEEPER IS COMMITTED

TO REACHING BEYOND ANY RACIAL

AND DENOMINATIONAL BARRIERS

TO DEMONSTRATE THE POWER

OF BIBLICAL UNITY.

Core issue: unity
Key passage to review in your group: John 17:20-23

An amazing thing happened one Tuesday morning at the church I attend. I lead a men's group there that had started as a small group, but now we have as many as 200 men show up each week! The previous week, we were all talking excitedly about the upcoming PK clergy conference in Atlanta and what we could do to encourage our pastors to attend.

Then, on the morning in question and without any prompting, one man showed up with a homemade graphic on a large board. On the left was a list of men's names, one under the other. Next to the list was a column with the heading "Pledged," and beside that was a second column labeled "Paid."

Whose were the names on the board? Try every pastor in our church (eight of them!), and then eight additional names of inner-city pastors and staff who wanted to go to the conference. Each of those 16 men needed financial assistance to attend.

That morning, we talked and prayed about providing that assistance, and then we put check marks first in column one, and eventually in column two, beside *every* name on the list. That meant sending 16 men—paying for their hotel, airfare, registration, and food—to an event that turned out to be a life-changing experience for them and for us.

The Tuesday after the clergy conference, all the pastors showed up at our meeting. We heard stories of relationships that had been built, barriers that had come down, and strategic ways that these churches and pastors had decided to link up in the months ahead. It was one of the most powerful times I've ever witnessed of seeing men of different colors and backgrounds come together and bond around the person and ministry of Jesus Christ.

A godly man is committed to biblical unity.

There's no doubt about it; God is no respecter of persons. He sees no Jew or Greek; no freeman or slave; no male or female; no black, white, red, or yellow. We are all one in Jesus Christ. But let's face it: Such color blindness is a distant dream in many communities and churches.

Often for what are called "good" reasons, racial or denominational differences aren't a basis for unity but for disharmony and strife. Without a doubt, those walls of distrust and discrimination are one of the most powerful barriers to oneness that the Christian church faces. But working to tear down those walls is an outstanding way for the reality of God's love to be broadcast in a hurting, hate-filled world.

When we can set aside differences and put our focus on loving Jesus Christ and each other, no matter what our color or tradition, we're demonstrating Christlike love.

Don't get me wrong. That's not to say a godly man is a universalist or that he ignores the clear teaching of Scripture for the sake of unity. People can be sincere about a false or unbiblical teaching—sincerely wrong. But a godly man has a biblical goal. It's actually the desire Jesus expressed for His disciples in John 17 when He told the Father, "I pray . . . that all of them may be one, Father, just as you are in me and I am in you. . . . May they be brought to complete unity to let the world know that you sent me and have loved them even as you have loved me" (verses 20, 21, 23).

A godly man recognizes the place for distinctions.

Distinctions are real. For example, it's not enough for someone to just "believe in God." We're told in Scripture, "Even the demons believe that—and shudder" (James 2:19). But a godly man seeks to major on the majors—things like the gospel message that Jesus died for our sins, was buried, and rose the third day according to the Scriptures—and avoid such irrelevancies as the color of another man's skin. He promotes major concerns like worshiping the Lord in spirit and truth and doesn't get hung up on whether our hands are raised or our heads are bowed.

Our common ground is Christ Jesus crucified, the only payment for our sin, the one whose sacrifice was a free gift to all who would believe (see John 3:16). Thus, while there are legitimate differences between denominations, those differences are bridged by the love of Christ.

A godly man sees the enrichment provided by diversity.

If you have any doubt that diversity is a key part of the Body of Christ, look closely at the book of 1 Corinthians. There we're told that there are many parts of the Body, and that each, though different, is indispensable.

"The body is a unit, though it is made up of many parts; and though all its parts are many, they form one body. . . . And if the ear should say, 'Because I am not an eye, I do not belong to the body,' it would not for that reason cease to be part of the body. If the whole body were an eye, where would the sense of hearing be?" (1 Corinthians 12:12, 16-17; see verses 12-31).

I've stood in the Superdome in New Orleans and seen black and white men embrace with tears in their eyes. Men who had never before touched a man of another color were standing arm in arm, worshiping Jesus. I've talked to people of different denominations in Oakland, California, who got past the minor issues to see a clear love for Jesus Christ that bonded them together. I've had the privilege of standing with a dozen men in Memphis and praying over a chain-smoking alcoholic who had just put his faith in Jesus and was now a brother in Christ.

Coming together around the person and work of Jesus Christ is a clear demonstration of what the Lord told the disciples in the Upper Room: "A new command I give you: Love one another. As I have loved you, so you must love one another. By this all men will know that you are my disciples, if you love one another" (John 13:34-35).

Expect this promise area to be one of the most challenging to live out. But watch how men committed to Christ can transform cultural, ethnic, and denominational differences in an incredibly powerful witness to God's love.

LIVING IT OUT

There weren't a lot of blacks where Fred grew up. The most frequent targets of racism were Hispanics. "The term 'dirty Mexican' was a frequent part of west Texas vocabulary," Fred admits. "And it was always 'Mex-can' rather than 'Mex-i-can.'"

The majority of students at Fred's high school had Hispanic heritage. Yet he says he never considered himself in the minority: "I was white, after all." He knew and got along well with many Hispanic kids at school—competing with them in sports, playing in the band with them, belonging to the same honor society, and serving together on the student council. But those relationships always seemed to begin and end at school.

An exception took place one day when a group of guys Fred hung out with walked to his house for lunch. He'd offered the spur-of-the-moment invitation without stopping to realize one of the guys was Hispanic. "I remember feeling uncomfortable the whole time he was at my house," Fred says. He continued to be friends with that boy and other Hispanics at school. But the experience reinforced the lesson in his mind: "It was clearly more comfortable for all concerned to stick with people of their own race. I never thought that was a matter of prejudice so much as it seemed simple common sense. It was just the way things were."

Fred certainly didn't consider himself bigoted. He even dated a Hispanic girl during college, though he could never forget their ethnic differences—at least for long. First it was his parents' disapproval: "We trust you aren't going to get serious with her. Surely you'll find another girlfriend soon."

The girl, too, kept reminding him of their differences. When they argued or she got upset about something, she'd say things like "You're too good for that— you're a white boy" or "You wouldn't understand because you live on the other side of town."

"I saw in her bitterness, for the first time, the deep pain caused by racial and ethnic differences," Fred says.

In many ways, Fred left his roots and broadened his perspective during his college years. He told himself his education and exposure to fellow students of many races during his medical-school days gave him a more enlightened view-point. As a committed Christian, he recognized as sin the kind of overt bigotry he'd seen in his family. But he didn't consider himself prejudiced anymore—if he ever was.

When he went to the Promise Keepers 1993 conference in Boulder, however, Fred became convicted by the speakers who talked about the need for Christian men to knock down the racial barriers that divide America. He realized that even though he thought he was free of the blatant intolerance that had been part of his cultural background, many barriers remained. At least in part, that was because he didn't really know or interact on a meaningful level with anyone of another race.

In response to the challenge, when Fred returned home to Dallas, he organized a Promise Keepers group of five men that included two blacks. "If I was going to knock down the racial barriers in my life," he says, "I knew I would need to under-stand from these two men their culture, their pain, and their love for Christ."

One of the men made an immediate and lasting impact on Fred. "I remember the first time we got together and I listened to Ernest talk," Fred says. "He began by shaking his head and saying, 'Oh, if my father could only see me now. This is something I have only dreamed of—to be able to share and pray with a white man.'

"And as Ernest began to reveal his heart, he started to cry. He told about the tough home life he had as a kid and how the military provided an escape. He'd had a substance-abuse problem for years before he found Christ. Now in his forties, he's a full-time counselor in a state hospital drug-rehab program. But he admitted he continues to struggle with the painful consequences of his past sins. His wife had divorced him when he was doing drugs and alcohol. So for years now, he's been working for reconciliation with the children he feels he failed as a father.

"The entire time Ernest talked, I felt like a little boy being led by the hand as this strong man of God opened up and showed me the power of Christ's love in his life. It created a longing in me to understand and spend more time with other minority men."

YOUR TURN

Having read an overview of promise six and Fred's story of trying to live it out, it's your turn to develop an initial plan of your own in this area by completing the forms that follow. Then transfer your plan to your daily planner/organizer.

CLOSING THE GAP

6

A Promise Keeper Is Committed to Demonstrating Biblical Unity

Personal Evaluation Point

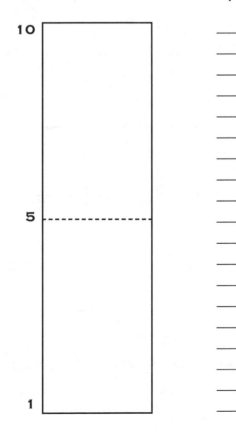

On a scale of 1 to 10, indicate by drawing a line where you stand in reference to promise six. Then fill in the area below the line.

Setting a Prayerful Horizon

Lord willing, 3 years from now my life will reflect this promise in these ways:

My age today _____

3 years from now _____

_____
_____
_____
_____
_____
_____
_____
_____
_____
_____
_____
_____
_____
_____
_____
_____
_____
_____
_____
_____

CLOSING THE GAP

Action Plan Worksheet

Knowing that I need to improve in this commitment, I will do my best to take a step of growth by following through in the three areas listed below:

1. *Action Point*

_____

_____

Potential Barrier

_____

_____

2. *Action Point*

_____

_____

Potential Barrier

_____

_____

3. *Action Point*

_____

_____

Potential Barrier

_____

_____

Accountability Commitment

Who _____

When _____

Now move your plan into the appropriate places in your daily planner.

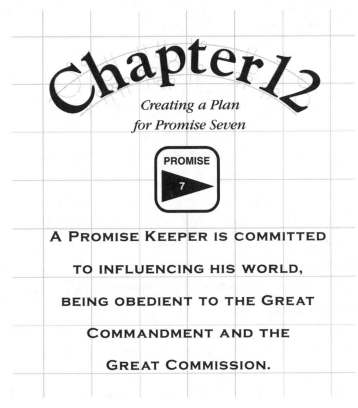

Chapter 12

*Creating a Plan
for Promise Seven*

**PROMISE
7** ▶

A Promise Keeper is committed to influencing his world, being obedient to the Great Commandment and the Great Commission.

Core issue: mission
Key passages to review in your group: Mark 12:30-31; Matthew 28:19-20

'll never forget the simple thing that led one young man in my Young Life club to Jesus Christ.

I had done my best to round up the kids who really needed to leave Texas and spend a week at Young Life's Frontier Ranch in Colorado. I had succeeded. The guys I'd collected were about 80 percent strongly non-Christian, and they were clearly going because it was 70 degrees in the mountains with no humidity, and there would be lots of good food and cute girls.

God does some amazing things in those mountains, as He had with me when I had gone to camp as a non-Christian years before. That was particularly true this time of a young man named Mark. And what happened that changed his life sheds clear light on this seventh promise of a Promise Keeper.

A godly man seeks to keep the Great Commandment.

Mark was much like me. He came from a single-parent home. Because of his dad's deserting the family, Mark had a problem trusting adults (especially men) and was coming to camp for the fun, not to meet Jesus Christ. But meet Him he did, and in a most unusual way.

The speaker that week was a man named Bob Mitchell. "Mitch" was one of the first Young Lifers. One day he would become president of the ministry, but at the time he was still a regional director.

Imagine several hundred high school kids at mealtime—loud, often obnoxious, the guys making every heaping platter disappear in seconds. But God was doing something miraculous at those meals.

During camp, the speaker was also the person who made the final decisions on the daily program. That included the time and place (indoors or out) for meals. And that's why the cook would come talk with Mitch during each meal to make sure she was on the right page.

The cook was a lady who obviously enjoyed her work with kids, but she also looked spent when she came to Mitch's table. Perhaps that was why, each time she came out to talk with him, Mitch would stand up, put her in his chair, and then let her get a moment's rest while they discussed the meal plans.

To my knowledge, no one—including me—noticed Mitch doing this . . . except for one person: Mark.

Mark hadn't come to hear anything about Jesus. But when he saw Jesus' love lived out in that simple act of kindness by the camp speaker, he began to listen to his talks. And on the last night of camp, he revealed that he had trusted Jesus as his Lord and Savior. It wasn't because of the messages, he said, but because of the love he saw in Bob Mitchell.

"If that's what it means to be a Christian," he said, "I want to be one."

Bob Mitchell and other men like him who change people's lives are men who live out the Great Commandment. It's found in Mark 12:28-31. When asked by one of the teachers of the Law, "Of all the commandments, which is the most important?" Jesus answered, "The most important one . . . is this: 'Hear, O Israel, the Lord our God, the Lord is one. Love the Lord your God with all your heart and with all your soul and with all your mind and with all your strength.' The second is this: 'Love your neighbor as yourself.' There is no commandment greater than these."

That's the kind of love Bob Mitchell demonstrated for God and, even more visibly, for that cook, and the life of one lost young man was forever changed.

A godly man is committed to the Great Commission.

The Great Commission is found in some of Jesus' last words to the disciples before He ascended to heaven. He told them (and all His disciples ever since, including us), "Therefore go and make disciples of all nations, baptizing them in the name of the Father and of the Son and of the Holy Spirit, and teaching them to obey everything I have commanded you" (Matthew 28:19-20).

When you say the word *missions,* people often get mental images of out-of-focus slides being shown by someone with a shrill voice, or of calls for money. But while we need to honor and support our missionaries, providing the funds to send them out, there's far more to missions than that. God calls on *each* of us to be involved personally in taking the message of the gospel to all corners of the world.

For some of us, it might mean supporting a missionary not just with our dollars, but also with our prayers and letters or E-mails of encouragement. (Thousands of missionaries are now linked to the Internet and love to get E-mail.) For others, there's no doubt that God is tapping them on the shoulder to go in person. And all of us have friends, neighbors, loved ones, and co-workers who need to hear the good news of God's love and see it lived out by us.

The Great Commandment and Great Commission are worthy of entire books of their own. However, I'll just take you back to those verses in Mark and Matthew. Those words were spoken to all believers by Jesus, and they come down to us as a sacred inheritance.

As Billy Graham often says, "There are no second-generation Christians." God's kingdom is going to be advanced in our families, communities, and world only if we get involved today.

LIVING IT OUT

I, Luis Palau, once lived next door to a young television personality. We would chat from time to time, and he mentioned that he listened to my Christian radio program occasionally. But I didn't present the gospel to him. *He seems completely immune to the problems of life,* I thought. He was a playboy type who lived "the good life." He didn't seem to care about spiritual values at all.

This neighbor eventually married a bright college graduate. After his wedding, everything still seemed to be going great for him. He and his wife would leave for work together, laughing and talking.

Suddenly, though, he changed. The joy seemed to have left his face. He and his wife started driving separate cars to work. I could tell their marriage was souring, and I felt the need to talk to him, but still I didn't want to meddle in his life. I went about my business and headed off to preach in an evangelistic crusade in Peru.

When I returned home, I learned that my neighbor had killed himself. I was heartbroken. I knew I should have gone to him and urged him to repent and follow Jesus. But because of false courtesy—because I followed a social norm—I never did it.

Though my neighbor seemed carefree, his soul was hurting, and I'm sure he would have welcomed the Good News. From that experience, I learned not to allow politeness to keep me from telling others about Jesus.

YOUR TURN

Having read an overview of promise seven and Luis Palau's story of trying to live it out, it's your turn to develop an initial plan of your own in this area by completing the forms that follow. Then transfer your plan to your daily organizer.

CLOSING THE GAP

7

A Promise Keeper Is Committed to Influencing His World

Personal Evaluation Point

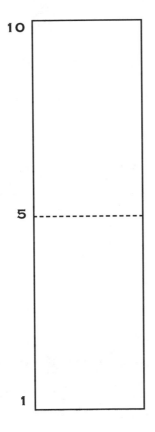 On a scale of 1 to 10, indicate by drawing a line where you stand in reference to promise seven. Then fill in the area below the line.

Setting a Prayerful Horizon

Lord willing, 3 years from now my life will reflect this promise in these ways:

My age today _____
3 years from now _____

_____
_____
_____
_____
_____
_____
_____
_____
_____
_____
_____
_____
_____
_____
_____
_____
_____
_____
_____
_____
_____

CLOSING THE GAP

$$\boxed{7}$$

Action Plan Worksheet

Knowing that I need to improve in this commitment, I will do my best to take a step of growth by following through in the three areas listed below:

1. *Action Point*

_____

_____

Potential Barrier

_____

_____

2. *Action Point*

_____

_____

Potential Barrier

_____

_____

3. *Action Point*

_____

_____

Potential Barrier

_____

_____

Accountability Commitment

Who _____

When _____

Now move your plan into the appropriate places in your daily planner.

Part III

The Making of a

GODLY MAN

purity
devotion
reconciliation
repentance

humility
servanthood
perseverance

LIVING OUT
YOUR PLAN

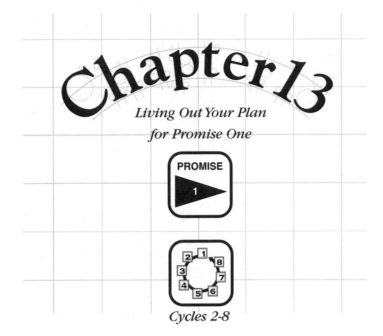

Chapter 13

Living Out Your Plan
for Promise One

Cycles 2-8

Now that you've created your spiritual growth plan, cycle through the promises so you can grow in your ability to live them out.

First, as a group, talk and pray about the order in which you should take the seven promises. Put your decisions in the chart below, writing the number of each promise in the appropriate flag:

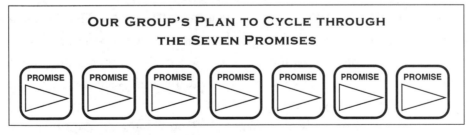

OUR GROUP'S PLAN TO CYCLE THROUGH THE SEVEN PROMISES

PROMISE PROMISE PROMISE PROMISE PROMISE PROMISE PROMISE

To cycle through each promise, you'll use each of the exercises in this and the following six chapters as the basis for a group session. Begin your group time in prayer, and then ask one another, "How have you lived out your plan this week?" and "What barriers have you faced or overcome?"

Next, following the directions in the exercise, use it as a springboard for discussion and application. In the final session for each promise, you'll "rest" by using your time to worship God, reflect on the progress you've made, and make any needed changes to your spiritual growth plan.

BASIC TRAINING AS YOU BEGIN THESE EXERCISES

As you and your group go through the various exercises in this chapter and the six that follow, you should understand that they're based on three basic aspects of the Christian life. On the next few pages, you'll find a description of a basic Bible study method, several essential elements of prayer, and a brief overview of the role and work of the Holy Spirit in your life. This is only an introduction to some deep and powerful truths, but as your group reads and talks through this section, it will give you a common ground of understanding.

1. A BASIC BIBLE STUDY METHOD

Throughout these exercises, you'll be asked to look up and study portions of God's Word. Here's some basic information to keep in mind:

Any time spent in God's Word is valuable.

The writer of the book of Hebrews said of God's Word, "For the word of God is living and active. Sharper than any double-edged sword, it penetrates even to dividing soul and spirit, joints and marrow; it judges the thoughts and attitudes of the heart" (Hebrews 4:12). Don't be surprised, therefore, when you read God's Word and find it "reading" you!

God's Word was written by men inspired by God's Holy Spirit, and as such, it's fully accurate and trustworthy. We read in 2 Timothy 3:16-17, "All Scripture is God-breathed and is useful for teaching, rebuking, correcting and training in righteousness, so that the man of God may be thoroughly equipped for every good work."

Finally, you'll never waste even five minutes in God's Word! We're told in the book of Isaiah, "So is my word that goes out from my mouth: It will not return to me empty, but will accomplish what I desire and achieve the purpose for which I sent it" (55:11).

Get a modern, readable translation of the Bible.

It's our suggestion that you get a good, readable *translation* of the Bible before you begin your small-group study and exercises—something like the NIV, NKJV, or NASB, not a paraphrase. Anyone at your local Christian bookstore will know the difference, for one is a translation of the Hebrew and Greek manuscripts in which the Bible was originally written, while the other is one man's interpretation of a translation. The Bible you pick doesn't have to have a leather cover or colored print. A plain version with easy-to-read type could be more helpful to you than one with a fancier cover.

If possible, get a Bible with a concordancc in the back.

A concordance is simply a "mini-dictionary" that can help you look up key words in the Scriptures. In the exercises that follow, several times you'll be asked to look up a key word (e.g., *servant*). A concordance allows you to quickly find several verses where that word is used.

Pick a quiet, comfortable place to study.

There's nothing to say you can't read your Bible in the lunchroom at work or on an airplane. However, we'd encourage you to keep your Bible and a notebook handy in a quiet, well-lit place. Consistency is the key, so if you have small children or are used to the television being on, you'll want to try to pick a time and place as free from distractions as possible.

As you read, write down key words that seem important, and feel free to ask questions a verse may raise.

One man, new to reading the Bible, read the Great Commission in Matthew 28. In his Bible, those powerful words of Jesus ended with the promise, "Lo, I am with you always, even to the end of the age" (NASB).

"Does that mean that the higher up we go, the less God is with us?" he asked.

We don't run into the Old English word *lo* very often, and he took it to mean "low." But by asking his question, he discovered the word meant "surely," and that it was safe to take a plane flight!

From a key term or word to a puzzling statement, give yourself permission to ask questions of your small group, or even of your pastor if necessary. Looking up verses or key words on your own is often a good way of learning more about God's Word.

2. KEY ELEMENTS OF PRAYER

Throughout these exercises, you'll be asked to pray for the other men in your group or about an attitude or character trait in your own life. If prayer is new to you, here are some important biblical basics to keep in mind:

Study the way Jesus taught the disciples to pray.

In Luke 11, an unnamed disciple made one of the most important requests Jesus ever granted: "Lord, teach us to pray."

What followed is called "the Lord's Prayer," and we'd highly encourage you to look it up and read it (see Luke 11:2-4). Entire books have been written about the Lord's Prayer, but let's focus here on four "P's" found in those verses.

Praise. Jesus began His prayer by telling the disciples to praise the Lord. "Father, hallowed be your name, your kingdom come." When you pray, begin by praising God for who He is and thanking Him for what He's done for you.

Provision. The Lord sanctified making prayer "requests" as He taught the disciples to pray, "Give us each day our daily bread." This realistic, honoring request of the Father is entirely appropriate. Ask God for those things that will allow you to do His will and be the person He wants you to be.

Petitions. The Lord next told the disciples to confess their sin: "Forgive us our sins, for we also forgive everyone who sins against us." Jesus was without sin, but we need to "wash" daily, admitting our sin and asking for God's forgiveness. First John 1:9 says, "If we confess our sins, he is faithful and just and will forgive us our sins and purify us from all unrighteousness." That's a new slate, a fresh start, each day when we confess our sins!

Protection. "And lead us not into temptation," Jesus prayed. So it's also appropriate to ask for the Lord's protection of your life, your family, and your friends. This can be protection from sin, or even physical protection.

Don't feel that these four P's lock you into a four-part formula that has to be followed slavishly in order for God to hear you. His Holy Spirit intercedes for us, even when we don't know the exact words to say. But you'll never go wrong praising God for who He is, asking for His legitimate provision for your needs, petitioning Him for the forgiveness of your sins, or asking for His protection from sin.

3. THE ROLE OF THE HOLY SPIRIT

God's Spirit has an essential place in the life and growth of a Christian.

Beginning in the Old Testament, we see that the Holy Spirit is a person, not just a "vapor" or indistinct being. He had a direct role in the creation of the world (see Genesis 1). He "filled" certain of God's people with extraordinary endowments (like King David and King Solomon). And in the New Testament, we see His role more clearly defined.

We're told in the book of Ephesians, "And you also were included in Christ when you heard the word of truth, the gospel of your salvation. Having believed, you were marked in him with a seal, the promised Holy Spirit, who is a deposit guaranteeing our inheritance until the redemption of those who are God's possession—to the praise of his glory" (1:13-14).

Jesus said that "promised Holy Spirit" would come to the disciples. He told them after He had risen from the grave, "But you will receive power when the Holy Spirit comes on you; and you will be my witnesses in Jerusalem, and in all Judea and Samaria, and to the ends of the earth" (Acts 1:8).

The Holy Spirit did indeed "fall" on the believers on the day of Pentecost, empowering them for the ministry ahead of them.

That empowering is available to believers today as well. The Holy Spirit is called our "paraclete," or Counselor, by the Lord (see John 14:16), and it's His role to fill the believer's heart with new capacities for love and service, and to convict us of our sin.

"Repent and be baptized, every one of you, in the name of Jesus Christ for the forgiveness of your sins," the apostle Peter said. "And you will receive the gift of the Holy Spirit. The promise is for you and your children and for all who are far off—for all whom the Lord our God will call" (Acts 2:38-39).

It's the Holy Spirit who helps us understand God's Word, who prays for us when we don't even know how to pray, and who works in our minds and hearts to bring about the lasting, godly change that we call "growing in Christlikeness."

Now, with these understandings of Bible study, prayer, and the work of the Holy Spirit, let's begin the exercises that will help you go deeper in your application of promise one of a godly man.

SESSION 1
HOW KINGDOM-MINDED ARE YOU?

One of the ways we honor God is by recognizing how and when He is at work in the world. This session's activity will help you to consider how you respond when things go right, as well as when things go wrong. Can you see God at work during both kinds of events? Answer questions 1 and 2 by yourself, and then discuss your responses with the other members of your group. Read and discuss number 3 together. Do number 4 as an assignment during the week.

1. How do you respond when things go right?

(Circle your response on the following scale.)

	Feel lucky/ I earned it			Give thanks to God		
a. Find a parking spot in the front row	1	2	3	4	5	6
b. See a beautiful sunset	1	2	3	4	5	6
c. Be invited to play golf	1	2	3	4	5	6
d. Receive a promotion	1	2	3	4	5	6
e. Get public praises from your boss	1	2	3	4	5	6
f. Find a bargain on a new tool	1	2	3	4	5	6
g. Have great weather on your vacation	1	2	3	4	5	6
h. Receive a salary increase and bonus	1	2	3	4	5	6

2. How do you respond when things go wrong?

(Circle your response on the following scale.)

	Gripe & complain			Trust that God knows best		
a. It rains on your golf game	1	2	3	4	5	6
b. You are passed over for promotion	1	2	3	4	5	6
c. A co-worker unfairly criticizes you	1	2	3	4	5	6
d. Your refrigerator quits working	1	2	3	4	5	6
e. You get stuck in rush-hour traffic	1	2	3	4	5	6
f. Your daughter needs braces	1	2	3	4	5	6
g. Your brakes must be overhauled	1	2	3	4	5	6
h. Your wife is in an accident	1	2	3	4	5	6

3. Read the following verses:

Matthew 5:45

Psalm 19:1

Romans 1:20

What do they say about God's activity in the world?

4. Look for one thing each day in the next week for which you can thank God. List the things you find in a few words below (e.g., "beautiful sunset" or "great worship service").

Monday: _____

Tuesday: _____

Wednesday: _____

Thursday:_____

Friday: _____

Saturday: _____

Sunday: _____

SESSION 2
ARE YOU PROUD OF THE GOSPEL?

This week's discussion focuses on how we react when the enemy has us in his sights. Do we wave our banner high and take our shots, or do we cower and hide? Read the following stories, and then discuss the questions that follow.

During the Civil War, it was a great honor to be chosen to carry the flag into battle. But with great honor came great danger! Since the enemy knew that your troops would rally around the flag, they often aimed for the flag bearer. Carrying the company's colors meant you were identified as a prime target. And yet, when the standard bearer was wounded or killed, other men would pick up the flag without hesitation.

As he commuted to work, Pete would listen either to a Christian radio station, Scripture on tape, or praise and worship tapes. One day he was taking a client, who was an avowed atheist and antagonistic to Christians, to lunch. Seeing the Christian tapes in the stereo, this person began to make fun of Pete for "wasting his time on myths and fables." Knowing how crucial this person's account was to his company, Pete wasn't sure how to respond.

How do these two stories relate to Paul's statement in Romans 1:16?

If you were Pete, how would you have responded?

Can you think of a time when being identified as a Christian made you a target of the enemy's attack? What happened? How did you feel about being a Christian? How would you respond now?

SESSION 3
DEALING WITH SIN

Each of us faces temptation daily. Sometimes we resist and stand firm. At other times, we stumble and fall. The secret to success in the Christian life is getting up after we've fallen. That may involve others' pointing out our sin and correcting us. This session looks at two men with vastly different responses to such correction. Read the Scripture passages aloud, and then discuss the questions that follow.

Saul   *1 Samuel 13:8-14; 15:1-3, 17-23, 27*
David   *2 Samuel 12:1-13*

Compare and contrast their responses.

	Saul	David
What sin(s) were they guilty of?		
Who confronted them?		
What were the consequences of their sin?		
How did they respond to the confrontation?		
Did they change after the confrontation? How?		

How does our response to correction reflect our walk with God?

Think of a time when you were confronted about sin in your life. How did you respond? If you could do it over again, what would you do differently?

SESSION 4
GOD'S LOVE AND YOUR FAMILY'S GROWTH

This session's activity will help you discover how well you and your family are understanding and modeling God's love. Do the exercise individually, and then discuss your thoughts as a group.

Psalm 103 is a wonderful poem that names at least 20 attributes of God's love. Some of those are things we can't duplicate. For instance, we can't be sovereign. But we *can* reflect many of His attributes to others. Those things are listed in the following chart. To complete this exercise:

1. Each person should read the psalm twice to become familiar with it.

2. Each person should evaluate how well his parents reflected these characteristics during his childhood. If they were consistent, place a check in the appropriate column ("M" for mother, "F" for father).

3. If you're married and/or a dad, in the "Me" column, put a check mark for each trait you believe you're consistently showing to your spouse and children. Then, using the "W" column, put a check mark for each trait you think your wife consistently displays to you and your kids.

4. Plan a special family time in which you discuss the first three columns with your family. Ask them how you can do better. Plan a separate time alone with your wife to discuss the "W" column.

OUR FATHER'S CHARACTERISTICS

| | Personalized | | Family | |
	M	F	Me	W
He pardons our sins				
He crowns us with lovingkindness and compassion				
He satisfies our desires with good things				
He does righteous things				
He helps those who are oppressed				
He makes His ways known				
He is compassionate and gracious				
He is slow to anger				
He is abounding in lovingkindness				
He doesn't stay angry with His children forever				
He doesn't deal with us according to our sins				
He has a father's compassion on those who fear Him				
His lovingkindness toward those who fear Him never ends..				

 **SESSION 5**
ALPHABET PRAISE

This week, honor God by praising Him for His character from A to Z. Do the brainstorming activity together, reminding each other of who God is and what He has taught you about Himself.

Brainstorm attributes or aspects of God's character that begin with each letter of the alphabet. See how many you can come up with. Here are a few to start your creative juices flowing:

A - almighty,

B -

C - Creator, creative,

D -

E - eternal

F - faithful, Father

G -

H -

I -

J - just, judge,

K -

L -

M -

N -

O -

P - protector, pure,

Q - quick,

R - righteous, Redeemer,

S -

T -

U -

V -

W -

X -

Y -

Z -

Meditate on one aspect of God's character each day this week. Look for ways that God demonstrates that attribute in your life. Don't forget to praise Him for it. Record your praises each day in three to five words:

_____

_____

_____

_____

_____

SESSION 6
KNOWING GOD BETTER

In order to praise and honor God, it's vital that we have an accurate view of who He is. Since His name reveals His character, studying His name will help you gain a better understanding of how He has revealed Himself to people throughout history. Read the following quotation, and then discuss the questions that follow.

> What comes into our minds when we think about God is the most important thing about us....The history of mankind will probably show that no people has ever risen above its religion, and man's spiritual history will positively demonstrate that no religion has ever been greater than its idea of God.... A right conception of God is basic not only to systematic theology but to practical Christian living as well. It is to worship what the foundation is to the temple; where it is inadequate or out of plumb the whole structure must sooner or later collapse. I believe there is scarcely an error in doctrine or a failure in applying Christian ethics that cannot be traced finally to imperfect and ignoble thoughts about God. (A. W. Tozer, "Why we must think rightly about God," in *The Knowledge of the Holy* [San Francisco: Harper & Row, 1961], pp.9-10)

Do you agree or disagree with the above quotation? Why?

How does our view of God affect our marriage? Job? Relationships with neighbors?

Look over the following names of God.

Jehovah Jireh, "the Lord will provide" (Genesis 22:14)

Jehovah Shalom, "the Lord is peace" (Judges 6:24)

Jehovah Rapha, "the Lord who heals you" (Exodus 15:26)

El Shaddai, "the almighty God" (Genesis 17:1)

El Elyon, "the most high God" (Genesis 14:19)

El Roi, "the God who sees" (Genesis 16:13)

Rock

Shield

Father

(For a more detailed list of the names of God, check out *Experiencing God,* by Henry Blackaby and Claude King.)

Pick one of the above names of God to study and meditate on this week. That means looking up the verse next to the name and reading how it's used in that context. Then reflect on what that name and characteristic of Almighty God mean in your life.

For example, Jehovah Jireh means "the Lord will provide" (Genesis 22:14). After reading the passage in Genesis, what do you think it means that the God of the universe is our "provider"? In what ways can you see how He's provided for you in the past? Do you need to trust Him to provide for you today? Do you stop at meals and throughout the day to thank Him for all He's provided by way of a church, friends, family, work, challenges, or faith? Write out your findings below:

✝ SESSION 7
WORSHIP AND REFLECTION

You've now spent six weeks going deeper into promise one. In this final session, spend the majority of your small-group time in prayer and worship to God. Thank Him for what He has accomplished in and through you so far, and ask for His help in continuing to grow and overcome any barriers that arise.

Finally, discuss with your group any changes you may need to make—based on your work over the last six sessions—in your plan for living out this promise. Record those changes, if any, below. Then transfer them to your daily planner/organizer.

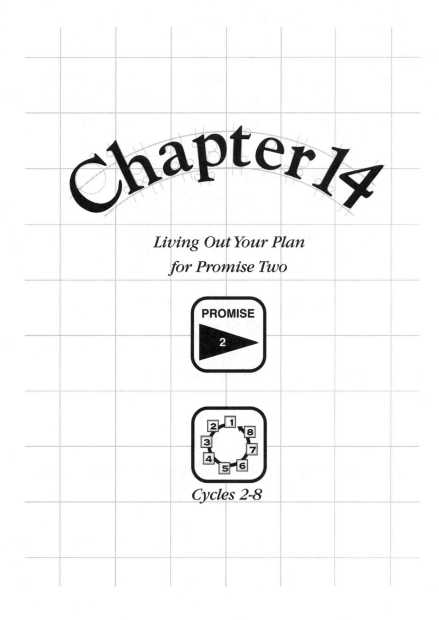

Chapter 14

Living Out Your Plan
for Promise Two

Cycles 2-8

SESSION 1
SOMEONE WHO BELIEVES IN YOU

As men, we grow up being taught to be independent and self-sufficient. Even though we need help to grow and reach our full potential, we resist or avoid it because of our upbringing. This session's activity will help you meet two men who benefited greatly from having a common mentor. Read the verses from Acts and 2 Timothy, and then discuss the questions that follow.

Acts 4:36-37; 9:26-27; 11:22-30; 13:7, 13; 15:36-41
2 Timothy 2:2

Describe the relationship Barnabas had with Saul/Paul.

In what way was Barnabas's relationship similar or different with John Mark?

How were Paul and John Mark changed as a result of their time spent with Barnabas?

What might you conclude about some of the benefits of mentoring?

In Proverbs 18:1 we read, "He who separates himself seeks his own desire, he quarrels against all sound wisdom" (NASB). What does this verse have to say about isolating ourselves from others? In your own words, why do you think so many men choose isolation over relationship? What's the cost of such a choice?

SESSION 2
THE BENEFITS OF MENTORING

Still not convinced of the value of mentoring? This session, discover five benefits of being a mentor/adviser to another man. Read the paraphrase of Howard Hendricks's book, study the passage in Exodus, and then compare the two in order to see how one mentor helped a protégé become more effective.

In his book *As Iron Sharpens Iron*, Howard Hendricks lists five benefits of being a mentor. He includes (1) a close relationship with another man, (2) personal renewal, (3) a sense of fulfillment, (4) enhanced self-esteem, and (5) an impact through your life.

Read Exodus 18:1-27. In what ways do you think Jethro experienced each of these benefits by mentoring Moses?

1. A close relationship

2. Personal renewal

3. A sense of fulfillment

4. Enhanced self-esteem

5. An impact

If you're not a mentor to someone already, which of those benefits appeal to you and challenge you to consider becoming one? Whom might you consider mentoring? Who could mentor you? Write some possible names below, and pray about these possibilities in the coming week.

How wise we become is directly related to how open we are to the counsel and correction of those closest to us. Since the book of Proverbs talks much about this subject, this session's activity will center in chapter 1. Read the passage, and talk about the different types of people Solomon described. Then rate your receptivity using the scale below. Do it individually, and then discuss your answers with the men in your group.

Read Proverbs 1:20-23.

The book of Proverbs identifies four different kinds of people. Which one would you like to be?

- naïve—aimless; inexperienced; drifting into temptation and even courting it. The naïve, or simple, needs to accept the discipline offered by the school of wisdom.

- scoffer—dislikes correction; deliberate troublemaker; bad influence. Mental attitude, not mental capacity, classifies a closed mind.

- fool—dull; obstinate; lazy. Wants wisdom handed to him rather than having to search for it. The root of his trouble is spiritual, not mental. His mind is closed, at least for the present, to God. Thus, he has rejected the first principle of wisdom, the fear of God. He's a menace to others.

- wise—listens to advice and counsel from others. Accepts discipline. Has a humble reverence for God.

Since one key to becoming wise is to listen to the counsel of others and accept discipline and correction, rate yourself on the following scale to discover how receptive you are to such counsel. Respond to each statement as honestly as you can by circling the appropriate number.

1 = Strongly agree

2 = Agree

3 = Undecided

4 = Disagree

5 = Strongly disagree

1. I have a difficult time admitting when I'm wrong.   1   2   3   4   5

2. Asking for help or directions is tough for me.   1   2   3   4   5

3. People don't understand my problems enough
   to be able to give me advice.   1   2   3   4   5

4. I look for people who will agree with my
   solutions when I have a problem.   1   2   3   4   5

5. When people disagree with me, I stop
   talking to them.   1   2   3   4   5

6. I seldom ask the advice of others.   1   2   3   4   5

7. I've had some painful experiences because
   I didn't listen to the counsel of others.   1   2   3   4   5

8. I have more wisdom than my friends. They
   should be coming to me for advice rather
   than me going to them.   1   2   3   4   5

9. I would rather teach than learn from others.   1   2   3   4   5

10. I would rather make a mistake than ask for help.   1   2   3   4   5

Scoring summary

10 - 20   Danger! Watch out for a prideful fall.

21 - 30   Clean your ears and learn to listen.

31 - 40   You're making progress toward wisdom.

41 - 50   You have surrounded yourself with wise friends.

For those men who scored 30 or less on this instrument, here are four suggestions for increasing your receptivity to counsel and correction:

1. Realize that God resists the proud and values a humble heart.

In the book of James, we're told, "God opposes the proud but gives grace to the humble" (4:6).

Think long and hard about that verse. Almighty God Himself says He stands in the way of the person who is proud, but He actively gives His favor to those who are teachable and humble. You're setting yourself against God when you stiffen your neck to godly correction.

2. Understand that God can and does use others to convict and confront us.

Read Numbers 22 in your Bible if you have any question about what the Lord can use to convict a man. There, it was a proud man named Balaam, and God used a donkey to get his attention and humble him! Whether it's your wife, children, a subordinate at work, or your pastor, God can and does use others to convict and confront.

3. Keep short accounts to keep your heart soft.

First John 1:9 tells us that if we confess our sins, God is faithful to forgive us. Unfortunately, unconfessed sin in a man's life is like quick-setting cement. That's why, for example, the Lord commands in Ephesians 4:26-27, "Do not let the sun go down while you are still angry, and do not give the devil a foothold." If you find it difficult to accept counsel and instruction, you can be almost certain you've got areas of sin you haven't confessed or dealt with in your life.

4. Find a friend who seems open to correction—and take lessons!

No one likes to be disciplined. Hebrews tells us, "No discipline seems pleasant at the time, but painful. Later on, however, it produces a harvest of righteousness and peace for those who have been trained by it" (12:11). That's the key. Find a man who is teachable and open to correction and you've usually found someone who sees the value in being honest. Sit down with that person, and ask him for help to grow in this area. It may be a humbling experience for you, but others have probably noticed your need anyway! Wise men seek counsel and advice. Don't you hesitate to do so.

SESSION 4
APPRENTICESHIP 101

If we're honest, none of us got to where we are without at least a little help. And as much as we hate to admit it, we're going to need even more help if we want to achieve our goals in the future. To help you think through this idea, read the following article on apprenticeship, and discuss the questions that follow with your group.

> Apprenticeship, system of learning the skills of a craft or trade from experts in the field by working with them for a set period of time. The apprenticeship system was used extensively by the craft guilds in the Middle Ages. It continued to be important in learning a trade until the Industrial Revolution in the 18th century, after which it was largely replaced by the factory system. Revived in the 20th century, it is used in the United States by industries that require highly skilled workers. The terms of modern apprenticeships are specified in a contract and are regulated by trade unions and laws. The National Apprenticeship Act passed in 1937 led to the establishment of the Bureau of Apprenticeship and Training in the U. S. Department of Labor, which works with employers, labor groups, and schools to promote apprenticeship programs. ("Apprenticeship," Microsoft ® Encarta. Copyright © 1994 Microsoft Corporation. Copyright © 1994 Funk & Wagnall's Corporation.)

Most of us have never entered into a formal apprenticeship. But each of us has learned skills necessary for success and survival at home and on the job. In regard to the following skills, who taught them to you, and what did you learn from them?

Skill	Whom did you learn it from?	What did you learn?
On-the-job skills		
Résumé writing		
Being a good husband		
Being a good father		
Communication (good listening habits)		
Financial management		
Making wise decisions		
Spiritual disciplines (Bible study, prayer, etc.)		
Ministry skills (sharing your faith, leading a small group, etc.)		

In which of the above areas could you use some additional training?

Whom do you know that you could ask to "apprentice" you in that area?

Set a time this week to call the person(s) and talk about it.

SESSION 5
RANGER BUDDIES

This week, think about the people who have been Ranger buddies to you, as defined below. You'll be encouraged to write letters and express your feelings to them. Do the assignment individually. While you don't need to read your letters to the others in your group, it would be profitable to tell them about your Ranger buddies and why you feel the way you do about them.

In chapter 6 of *Go the Distance,* Stu Weber describes a Ranger buddy as a man who will:

• stick with you
• never leave you
• encourage you
• carry you through difficult times

He's a buddy, a fellow soldier, a mentor to walk beside you in the swift-flowing challenges of life.

With that definition in mind, who (if anyone) have been your Ranger buddies in the past? Is there another man whom you would call your Ranger buddy *today?* Take the time now to write them letters expressing your gratitude for what they've meant to you.

If you don't have a Ranger buddy, perhaps there's a man in your church or small group whom you can team up with to "go the distance" for God. Make a list of men who could be such a friend. If you still come up with a blank, ask the Promise Keepers Key Man in your church, your men's ministry leader, or your pastor for suggestions. In your small group, discuss steps that two men can take to begin developing a Ranger buddy-level of friendship.

SESSION 6
THE MINISTRY OF MULTIPLICATION

Mentoring, rather than being a single-point-in-time event, is an ongoing cycle of receiving help and encouragement from someone and then passing it on to someone else. As a group, read the statement from Howard Hendricks below, and then discuss the questions that follow. You'll be challenged to think about those who have mentored you, as well as those whom you can pour your life into.

> Every man here should seek to have three individuals in his life. You need a Paul. You need a Barnabas. And you need a Timothy. . . . [T]hese are three kinds of mentoring relationships that a man desperately needs to pursue: a Paul, an older man who can build into his life; a Barnabas, a peer, a soul brother to whom he can be accountable; and a Timothy, a younger man into whose life he is building. (Howard Hendricks and William Hendricks, *As Iron Sharpens Iron* [Chicago: Moody, 1995], p.78)

Using the questions below, reflect on your own need to be led by an older man, encouraged by a peer, and instrumental in developing a younger man. (One of those three might also become your Ranger buddy.)

1. Think about the locations where you might discover a potential mentor: office, church, small group, family, social gatherings, civic clubs, etc.

2. In each of these places, identify the key people who are able to open the door to the right mentor.

3. Based on your conclusions, who might be an older and more experienced "Paul" who could mentor you? Evaluate the potential individuals.

4. Think through the possible "Barnabas" men—the soul brother who might serve as a peer in a mutual encouragement arrangement. Who's in a situation similar to yours?

5. Identify your possible "Timothys"—younger men into whom you might pour your life and experience. With whom might you share your wisdom and guidance?

6. In your small group, talk about whom you came up with as possibilities for a Paul, a Barnabas, and a Timothy, as well as practical ways to pursue those relationships.

✝ SESSION 7
WORSHIP AND REFLECTION

You've now spent six weeks going deeper into promise two. In this final session, spend the majority of your small-group time in prayer and worship to God. Thank Him for what He has accomplished in and through you so far, and ask for His help in continuing to grow and overcome any barriers that arise.

Finally, discuss with your group any changes you may need to make—based on your work over the last six sessions—in your plan for living out this promise. Record those changes, if any, below. Then transfer them to your daily planner/organizer.

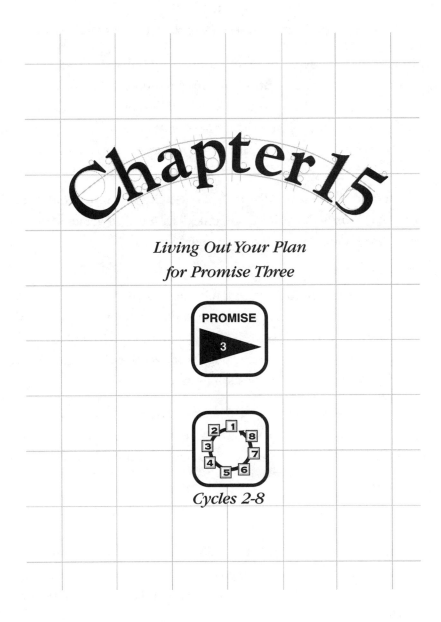

Chapter 15

Living Out Your Plan
for Promise Three

Cycles 2-8

SESSION 1
CAN YOUR LIFE SURVIVE AN EARTHQUAKE?

We read much about being prepared for a natural disaster such as an earthquake, tornado, or hurricane. Part of that preparation involves taking an honest look at where we are. In this session, take a hard look at your personal life to see how rock-solid you are. Answer the questions in the inventory by yourself before discussing them with the men in your group. Then name one area in which you'd like to see growth this week, and ask the other men to pray for you.

Complete and discuss the "Trent-Hicks Stability Inventory" (adapted from *Seeking Solid Ground,* by John Trent and Rick Hicks) to get an idea of where you are in developing a rock-solid character.

How to Take This Inventory

Read each question through completely and thoughtfully. It helps if you can relate it to a real-life situation. Then circle the number below that best represents how you would actually respond in that situation. Remember to answer honestly, as you really are today, not with what you think is right or how you would like to be. Answer each question on a 1 to 7 scale.

PART I: ANCHORING OUR PERSONAL LIVES INDEX

1. When you talk to people, are your comments sincere, or do you sometimes put on a front, speaking in such a way as to create a misleading impression?

Struggle with sincerity   *Always sincere*

| 1 | 2 | 3 | 4 | 5 | 6 | 7 |

2. You've just received a second reimbursement check for the same business trip. You know your company's bookkeeping process, and there's no way they can trace this back to you once you cash it. How difficult would it be for you to not cash the check?

Real difficulty in not cashing it   *Absolutely wouldn't*

| 1 | 2 | 3 | 4 | 5 | 6 | 7 |

3. When someone does something that really offends you, how difficult is it for you to forgive the person?

Difficult to forgive   *Desire to forgive*

1   2   3   4   5   6   7

4. The programs you watch on television . . .

Frequently watch violent/suggestive shows   *G-rated TV habits*

1   2   3   4   5   6   7

5. Do you make a habit of doing "first things first," or do urgent but relatively unimportant things fill your day?

Urgency dictates my day   *Focused on what's important*

1   2   3   4   5   6   7

6. Is it difficult for you to accept that faith alone is what qualifies you for God's presence?

Feel I need to earn my relationship with God   *Life based on faith alone*

1   2   3   4   5   6   7

7. By honest evaluation, do you use "little lies" at work?

Struggle with "little lies"   *Always speak truthfully*

1   2   3   4   5   6   7

8. When you hit times of trial, do you typically tell yourself, "I'm still valuable in God's eyes" or "Perhaps God is punishing me or isn't with me"?

Struggle feeling acceptable to God   *Never question His acceptance*

1   2   3   4   5   6   7

PART II: PROTECTING OUR MOST IMPORTANT RELATIONSHIPS INDEX

9. If you're frustrated by someone, how likely are you to exaggerate a story to put the person in a bad light?

I do this often   *I wouldn't do it*

1   2   3   4   5   6   7

10. If you're offended by, wronged by, or dislike someone, do you find yourself looking for opportunities to discredit the person?

Always   *Never*

1   2   3   4   5   6   7

11. When put in a situation where seeking your desires infringes on someone else's well-being, how much do you consider the negative effect it will have on the other person?

I have my rights; others'   *The well-being of others is an*
well-being is not my concern   *important consideration for me*

1   2   3   4   5   6   7

12. There's a person who has a history of making life difficult for you. You're now in a situation that would give you a chance to get even. How likely is it that you'll take advantage of this opportunity?

I'll do it in a heartbeat   *In spite of everything, I won't hurt someone else*

1   2   3   4   5   6   7

13. At work, if you heard something negative about a co-worker, would you be likely to believe it right away or reserve judgment until you could investigate further and discern the truth?

Believe the worst   *Give the benefit of the doubt*

1   2   3   4   5   6   7

14. Are you likely to abandon or remain loyal to a friend who has failed or is wrong in some situation?

Abandon   *Remain loyal*

1   2   3   4   5   6   7

PART III: GUIDING OUR PUBLIC WALK INDEX

15. Are you inclined to make fun of other Christians whose beliefs, worship styles, or personalities are different from your own?

Inclined to make fun a lot   *Not inclined to make fun*

1   2   3   4   5   6   7

16. Whom do you find yourself more impressed and influenced by?

Society's celebrities   *Individuals with godly character*

1   2   3   4   5   6   7

17. You've made a commitment to someone, and later you get a better offer. What's your response?

Do what's best for me   *Keep my promise*

1   2   3   4   5   6   7

18. How confident are your family and friends that you will fulfill your promises to them?

They believe it when they see it   *They know my word is my bond*

1   2   3   4   5   6   7

19. You book a flight for a business trip with an airline that uses your personal frequent flyer miles. Your company will reimburse you for the airfare. You could have saved your company money by booking a cheaper flight on a different airline. In a situation like this, how likely would you be to charge your company only for the lowest price you could have booked?

Very unlikely   *A sure thing*

1   2   3   4   5   6   7

20. You have a chance to take advantage of a profitable financial opportunity. You're also aware that going through with it will cause difficulties for several other people. How much do the ramifications for others influence your decision?

I don't give them much thought   *They greatly influence my decision*

1   2   3   4   5   6   7

PART IV: MAINTAINING SEXUAL PURITY

21. Martin Luther once said concerning temptation, "You can't keep birds from flying over your head, but you can keep them from building a nest in your hair." This past week, how often has your mind dwelled on a sexually impure thought once it has popped into your mind?

Frequent thoughts (more than once a day)   *Very infrequent*

1   2   3   4   5   6   7

22. When faced with sexual temptation, how easy is it for you to flee vs. falling? (Falling equals acting out or staying to watch something you shouldn't; fleeing means quickly turning the station or moving away to do something more constructive.)

Fall nearly every time   *Flee consistently*

1   2   3   4   5   6   7

23. As a young man (teenage years and early twenties), how heavy an exposure to pornography did you have?

Great deal of exposure   *Little exposure*

1   2   3   4   5   6   7

24. Today, how satisfied are you with the level of personal control and discipline you have in facing sexual temptation?

Feel I have little control   *Strong discipline*

1   2   3   4   5   6   7

Scoring

Total all the numbers you circled = _____

Mark your total score with an "X" on the line of numbers below.

Turbulent Lifestyle   *Stable Lifestyle*

24   40   65   80   100   120   140   168

Date_____

Six months from now, take the inventory a second time and compare your two scores to see if you've grown toward a more stable lifestyle.

 **SESSION 2**
THE MEASURE OF A MAN

Countless books and magazine articles have been written describing various qualities of manhood. While they may be helpful, we would be wise to measure ourselves against the standard of Scripture. Psalm 15 lists 10 qualities that describe what a man of God should look like. This week in your group, read Psalm 15 and discuss how to apply those qualities to your own life.

1. What question is David asking?

2. What do you think are some of the benefits of being welcome in God's house?

3. The three qualities in verse 2 are related to who we are in private. Think of someone from whose life these qualities are absent. How is his life affected?

4. Verse 3 describes three characteristics that affect our relationships with others. What benefits have you experienced when you've practiced these qualities?

5. Verses 4 and 5 list four qualities that are demonstrated in our public walk. Which one comes easiest for you? Which is the most difficult? Why is that?

6. Which of the 10 qualities in Psalm 15 do you most need to develop further? How can you do that, starting in the next week?

SESSION 3
BECOMING MEN OF INTEGRITY

In the last session, you discovered several qualities of Christian manhood. Some have suggested that they could be summed up in one word, *integrity*. This session, focus your time on developing your own definition of integrity, and talk about what it looks like in daily life.

• Webster defines *integrity* as (1) soundness; (2) adherence to a code of values: utter sincerity, honesty, and candor; (3) completeness.

• One person defined *integrity* as who you are when no one is looking.

• Another man defined *integrity* as authenticity from the core to the crust.

• Still another man described *integrity* as character in the dark.

As a group, talk through the meaning of integrity, and write out your own definition.

What does integrity look like in another person? What qualities does a man need to demonstrate for you to say, "He has integrity"?

Whom do you know that most fits that definition? When have you seen that integrity displayed?

What areas in your life do you need to shore up to match your definition of integrity? How will you begin to do that?

 **SESSION 4**
OWNING UP TO SEXUAL OPPRESSION OR ADDICTION

There's no doubt that the Lord wants each man to be sexually pure. There's also no doubt that this area of temptation presents one of the greatest struggles for most men.

Individually, read over the case study of Mike that follows. Then discuss it and the "Lust-Anger Cycle" with your small group. *In this area in particular, pray before your discussion for the courage to be brutally honest about this area of significant spiritual warfare.*

Case study — Falling instead of fleeing from sexual sin

"I can't believe it," Mike said, sobbing in his hotel room.

Once again, he had thought about how strong he was going to be on this business trip, and once again he had turned on the X-rated movies and spent several hours watching them.

"I hate myself!" he cried. "I'm so weak!"

He also knew that the next trip, he'd be all talk and likely to fall once more.

What's happening to Mike? For one thing, try the "lust-anger" cycle.

The Lust-Anger Cycle

Bob comes from a home where his father was passive, his mother dominant.

Bob and his wife argue often and have infrequent sexual relations.

Bob is under a great deal of stress at work, with little support from home.

Bob feels elation when watching an illicit movie.

Immediately afterward, Bob feels massive guilt over what he's done.

Bob goes home feeling worse about his life, marriage, and spiritual life.

Bob recalls his distance from his father, and anger toward his mother.

This cycle can repeat itself time and again:

Inner anger and lack of positive relationships

lead to acting out a lust episode,

which leads to massive guilt,

which leads to more inner anger and worse home relationships,

which leads to another lust episode to try to "feel" better,

which leads to more guilt,

which leads to worse relationships . . .

Group discussion questions

Honestly, do you face this cycle or something like it frequently?

What have you done/are you doing about breaking it?

What have you done in the past that has helped you stay sexually pure?

What can you do better the next time you face the temptation to use pornography?

SESSION 5
FINDING MODELS OF INTEGRITY

In this session, you will learn about a man who had to practice integrity in real life. Read the following story, and discuss the questions that follow with the members of your group.

Jason was a cement contractor in a large city. He learned that the city wanted to build a recreational water park that would include swimming pools, fountains, and several water slides. Jason and his company entered the bidding process and were awarded the contract. After signing the contract, he reread the specifications prior to ordering material and breaking ground on the park. To his dismay, he discovered that he had misread the specifications and had left out a large section of the park in estimating his bid. After adding in the cost for the extra material, he was horrified to learn that instead of turning a profit, he now stood to lose $200,000.

Jason's business partner said he should go back to the city and find a legal way to get more money or get out of the contract. Jason felt strongly that since he had signed a contract, he was morally obligated to fulfill the terms to which he had originally agreed.

What do you think Jason should do? Why?

What impact, if any, will your solution have on Jason's reputation?

How can he demonstrate integrity in this situation?

SESSION 6
SAYING NO TO TEMPTATION

It's easier to resist temptation when we know where it will strike and can shore up our defenses accordingly. This session's activity will help you to think through the areas where you're most vulnerable. As a group, read the passage and discuss the questions that follow.

Read 1 John 2:15-17.

John lists three crippling areas of temptation:

- Lust of the flesh (a strong craving or desire, especially sexual desire)
- Lust of the eyes (the sinful desire to possess whatever material good, position, or relationship someone else has)
- Pride of life (thinking and acting as if we alone—with our own indomitable soul—can determine our course of life apart from God)

In what ways are men tempted in each of these areas?

Think of some men who have fallen into sin in one or more of these areas. What has happened? What impact does it have on their families? Careers? Friendships?

It has been said that most of us go through life with chalk on our toes from standing too close to the lines we know we shouldn't cross. In which area are you most tempted to cross the line and give in? Why?

If you could ask for help from the men in your group to help you gain victory over this temptation, what would you ask for?

What else can you do to overcome temptation in each of the three areas mentioned in 1 John 2? What might be the "way out" promised in 1 Corinthians 10:13?

✝ SESSION 7
WORSHIP AND REFLECTION

You've now spent six weeks going deeper into promise three. In this final session, spend the majority of your small-group time in prayer and worship to God. Thank Him for what He has accomplished in and through you so far, and ask for His help in continuing to grow and overcome any barriers that arise.

Finally, discuss with your group any changes you may need to make—based on your work over the last six sessions—in your plan for living out this promise. Record those changes, if any, below. Then transfer them to your daily planner/organizer.

Chapter 16

*Living Out Your Plan
for Promise Four*

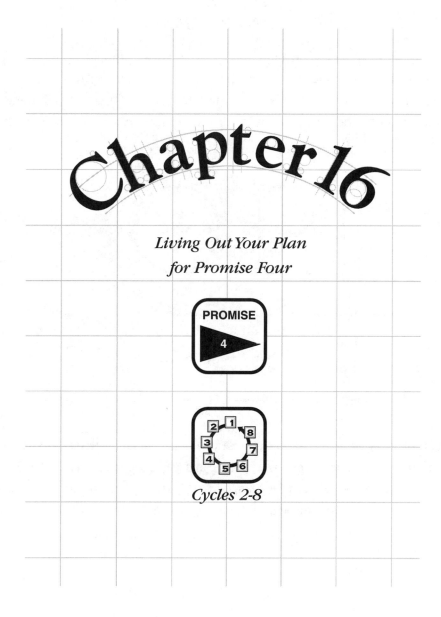

Cycles 2-8

SESSION 1
SCULPTING A FAMILY

To have a healthy family and a hopeful future, it helps to think through your past family relationships and how they shaped who you are today. The following family sculpting exercise will guide you in doing that. Think through the exercise on your own before discussing your responses with the men in your group.

Begin by graphing your family using the following example:

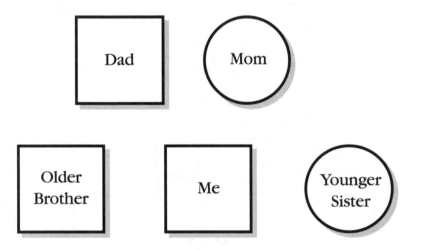

As you can see, this is a graphic representation of your family tree. Begin with your mother and father. (Men are in boxes, women in circles.) Then add in each child in your family, going from the oldest to the youngest. Once you've got the names of each family member, it's time to think through your past by answering the following questions:

In what ways are you like your father? In what ways are you different?

In what ways are you like your mother? In what ways are you different?

How close was your family physically? Did you touch frequently (hugs, back rubs, pats on the back, etc.)?

How close was your family emotionally? Did you share your feelings with each other?

What were your family's strengths?

What were your family's weaknesses?

Were there any unwritten family rules? (E.g., negative unwritten rules might be "Never show any weakness" or "We don't invite those types of people to our home.")

Were there any family ghosts, something everyone knew about but no one was allowed to mention?

Which of your birth family's strengths would you like to perpetuate in your family today? Which of its weaknesses and unwritten rules would you like to eliminate?

SESSION 2
BECOMING AN UNDERSTANDING HUSBAND

First Peter 3:7 tells husbands to "live with your wives in an understanding way" (NASB). But let's face it! As men, we need help in understanding women, especially our wives, daughters, sisters, and mothers. If you're married, sit down with your wife—if you're not married, with your sister, girlfriend, or another female friend—and ask the following questions. When you meet with your small group, discuss some of the things you learned.

1. What do you see as your strengths?

2. In what areas would you like to grow?

3. If you could spend a day any way you would like, what would you do?

4. What brings you joy?

5. What causes you to be sad?

6. If you could live anywhere in the world, where would that be, and why?

7. If you could talk with a famous person from history, who would it be, and what would you like to ask?

8. Where is your favorite vacation spot?

9. What is your favorite way to relax?

10. If you were to see God face to face, what's the first thing you would say to Him?

11. If you had to describe yourself to a stranger in only three words, what would you say?

12. What one goal would you most like to accomplish in the next 12 months?

13. How can I help you reach that goal?

14. What do you see as your spiritual gifts?

15. If God were to give you $1 million, how would you spend it?

16. If God were to give you $10, how would you spend that?

17. Tell me about your most memorable Christmas.

18. Whom did you admire most when you were a child? Why?

19. When do you feel most secure?

20. What can I do to help strengthen our relationship?

If you find you're enjoying the conversation so much that you don't want to stop, come up with some more questions of your own!

SESSION 3
A FAMILY COAT OF ARMS

How would you describe your family to a close friend? What qualities or characteristics make up your family? The following exercise will help you to think through those questions. Complete the activity as a family, and then discuss your picture with the men in your small group.

A coat of arms was originally used as a means of identifying knights in battle. Today, it serves to distinguish families, corporations, and even states and nations. The elements of a coat of arms draw on a rich vocabulary of symbols that are used to represent the identity of the bearer with accuracy and pride.

Using the shield below, draw a coat of arms for your family.

• In one quadrant, draw an animal that pictures your family's strengths.
• In the second quadrant, draw an activity that your family enjoys doing.
• In the third quadrant, write three words that describe your family.
• In the final quadrant, write or create your family's motto.

Here is one family's coat of arms as an example:

The Meier Family Coat of Arms

Quadrant one: A flock of ducks. (We view ourselves as a close family. We know that duck pairs bond for life. What's more, when migrating, they fly in formation, taking turns in the lead and helping to encourage one another.)

Quadrant two: A camping pop-up trailer. (When asked what activity everyone most enjoyed as a family, it was camping, hands down.)

Quadrant three: *striving/committed/loving* (Striving to please God in all we do. Committed to the Lord and each other. Loving each other and those around us as God first loved us.)

Quadrant four: God isn't finished with us yet. (We feel we've come far as a family. Yet we know that God isn't finished with us yet! We're in process, becoming the people and family He wants us to be.)

Now complete your family coat of arms in the shield on the next page.

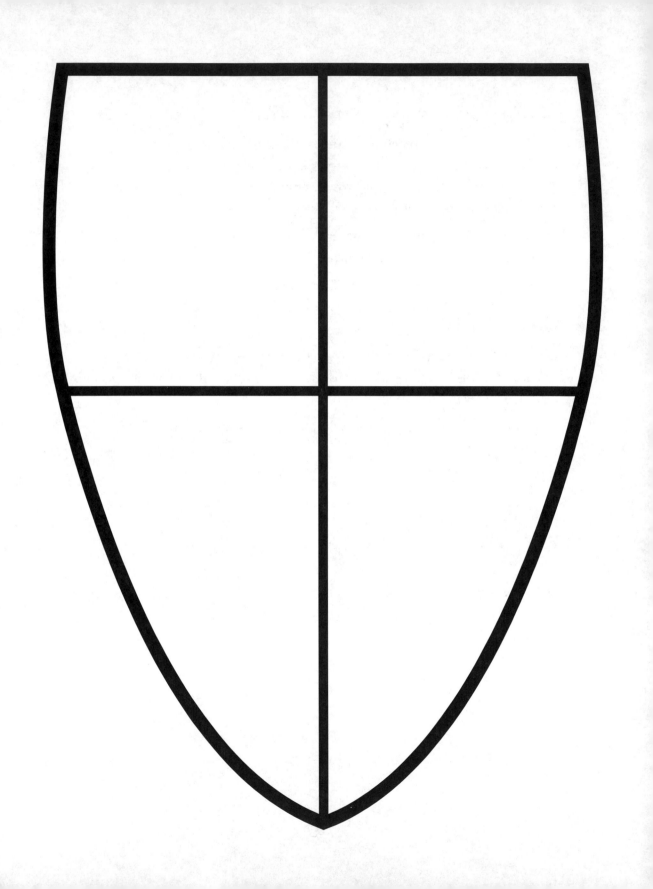

SESSION 4
SELFISHNESS AND SACRIFICE

In this session, you'll discover the degree to which you give up your rights or demand that they be met. Complete the activity on your own, and then ask for your wife's/children's input. Discuss what you learn about yourself with the men in your small group.

Being in a family sometimes requires putting others' needs ahead of your own. To help you discover the degree of your selfishness or sacrificial attitude, rate yourself on the following statements. Circle the appropriate, honest answer.

	Always			Never	
1. When watching TV, I choose what we watch.	1	2	3	4	5
2. At a restaurant, I order first.	1	2	3	4	5
3. When watching TV, I hang on to the remote control.	1	2	3	4	5
4. I pick the radio station in the car.	1	2	3	4	5
5. On vacation, we go to my choice of destination.	1	2	3	4	5
6. I'm upset when my needs aren't met.	1	2	3	4	5
7. I'm jealous of the time my wife spends with the kids.	1	2	3	4	5
8. I would rather spend money on my hobbies than let my wife spend the same amount on her hobbies.	1	2	3	4	5
9. I don't like to be interrupted while watching a football game.	1	2	3	4	5
10. When reading the paper, I don't put it down when my children/spouse want to talk to me.	1	2	3	4	5
11. When I have a day off, we spend it the way I want.	1	2	3	4	5
12. I would rather stay home and watch a football game than take my family to church on Sunday morning.	1	2	3	4	5
13. I would rather work overtime than spend an evening talking with my family.	1	2	3	4	5

For the brave of heart: Now that you've completed the survey, give it to your wife, and ask her to rate you on the same statements.

For the truly courageous: Give the survey to your children, and ask them to rate you as well.

SESSION 5
PRAISING YOUR WIFE

Most of us would not be where we are today without the encouragement, sacrifice, and help of our wives. But our gratitude often goes unsaid. This week, tell your mate how you feel in a letter, following the instructions below. Share only the high points of your letter with the men in your group.

Even if it's hard for you to do, write that letter to your wife. There's something incredibly powerful about spoken or written words of praise. Some ideas you might include:

• Praise her for her character. (E.g., "I've always admired your honesty.")
• Thank her for something she has done for you. (E.g., "Thanks for standing with me when I lost my job last year.")
• Express your gratitude for how she takes care of your children. (E.g., "You do a terrific job of making the kids feel loved and secure.")

SESSION 6
COFFEE CUP COUNSELING

This week in your group time, discuss how you would help another brother put his marriage back together, using the following story as your starting point.

At lunch one day, Joe explains that his marriage is on the rocks. He admits he has been extremely selfish, constantly putting his needs and wants ahead of his wife's. He has been verbally abusive, criticizing and belittling her in public. In addition, he has shirked his responsibility to be the leader in the home, forcing his wife to make decisions because he won't. He also reluctantly admits that while his wife has been growing spiritually, he has neglected his own Bible reading and prayer time for quite a while.

Now that his wife has threatened to leave him, he has recognized the error of his ways. But he doesn't know where to start to change. He's also afraid to try, because he has made promises to change before and has not followed through.

What counsel would you give Joe?

Moving from story to reality: As you look at your own marriage—particularly if you read this hypothetical story to your wife—how much would *she* say it sounds like your marriage? Are you facing some tough issues at home that you need to discuss with the men in your small group right now?

There's no better place to share hurts, fears, or failures than in a group of Christian men who love you and are committed to you. Make this a "gut check" session in which each of you openly shares his heart and the state of his marriage.

✝ SESSION 7
WORSHIP AND REFLECTION

You've now spent six weeks going deeper into promise four. In this final session, spend the majority of your small-group time in prayer and worship to God. Thank Him for what He has accomplished in and through you so far, and ask for His help in continuing to grow and overcome any barriers that arise.

Finally, discuss with your group any changes you may need to make—based on your work over the last six sessions—in your plan for living out this promise. Record those changes, if any, below. Then transfer them to your daily planner/organizer.

Chapter 17

Living Out Your Plan
for Promise Five

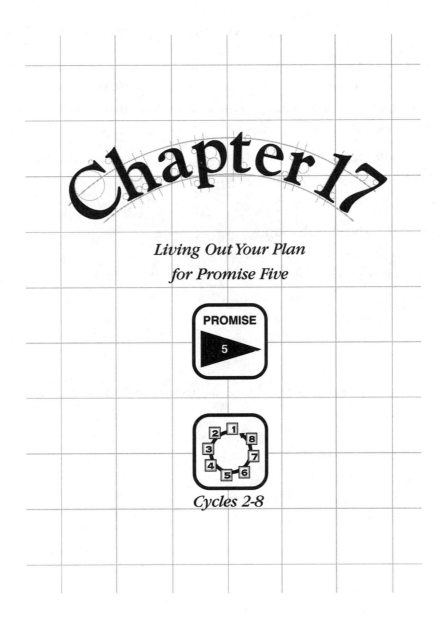

Cycles 2-8

SESSION 1
BECOMING YOUR PASTOR'S FRIEND, PART 1

The first two sessions in this promise area will focus on helping you get to know your pastor as a person so you can support and pray for him more effectively. For the next session's group meeting, you'll be encouraged to take your pastor out to lunch. During this session, develop a list of questions that you can ask him.

Brainstorm a list of questions to ask your pastor over lunch. Focus on getting to know him as a person. To help prime the pump, here are some starter questions. Add your own.

Get-to-know-you questions
1. What activities are your children involved in?
2. What are your hobbies?
3. How long have you been married?
4. Who are your heroes in ministry? Why?
5.
6.

Deeper questions (after you've developed a relationship with him)
1. What are your dreams for this church?
2. How can we help you reach your goals?
3. In what areas do you feel temptation?
4. What brings you joy?
5. What causes you sorrow in ministry?
6. How can we pray for you?
7.
8.

SESSION 2
BECOMING YOUR PASTOR'S FRIEND, PART 2

As a group, take your pastor out to lunch this week, and get to know him better.

Record briefly what you learned (two- or three-word phrases; e.g., "an avid golfer!"):

_____

_____

_____

_____

_____

_____

_____

_____

_____

Conclude your time with your pastor by praying for him.

SESSION 3
DEVELOPING A SENSE OF COMMUNITY

All of us want a place to belong. But true community is more than merely belonging. It's a place where reciprocal ministry occurs. This week you'll become acquainted with a passage of Scripture that describes such a place.

The New Testament uses the word *koinonia* to describe fellowship, association, community, communion, and joint participation. We develop a sense of community within a church by serving together, as well as by practicing the "one anothers." A key passage that describes both of these is Romans 12:1-21. Study this passage to discover God's instructions, and discuss how to put them into practice in your small group and church.

What does Scripture say?

Read Romans 12, and answer these questions:

1. (12:1) It has often been said, "The problem isn't with offering our bodies as living sacrifices—it's that we keep crawling off the altar!"

Why is it so difficult for us men to fully, completely give ourselves to God? What have you personally struggled with the most?

2. (12:2) The original New Testament Greek word translated "transformed" is *metamorpheo*. What's an example of a spiritual "metamorphosis," and why is this such a powerful picture of change?

3. (12:3-8) Discuss a modern example (from the sports or business world) of someone whose pride caused him to cross the line ethically or morally. Think about someone else whose "team attitude" makes him an invaluable asset to a sports or business team. How does looking at your talents as a gift help you to keep a proper perspective on life?

4. Paul's summary statement is in 12:21: "Do not be overcome by evil, but overcome evil with good." In a world that's growing increasingly hostile to the things of God, how do you keep from getting discouraged or "repaying evil for evil"?

How should we do this in our small group? In our church?

SESSION 4
HONOR ONE ANOTHER

In this session, you'll have the opportunity to practice the command to "honor one another." Discuss this activity as a group.

When we think of people to honor, it's easy to identify the folks who are up front and leading the way. But the ones who serve behind the scenes work just as hard yet receive much less, if any, recognition and honor.

Think about the people who serve in your church. Who is serving behind the scenes? What roles do they play? What ministries would be crippled if they abandoned their positions? Try to come up with a list of behind-the-scenes servants.

Next, pick one of the people and brainstorm some ways in which you can honor him or her this week.

People	Ways to show honor

SESSION 5
HOW INVOLVED ARE YOU IN THE MISSION
OF YOUR CHURCH?

This session, take an honest look as to how involved you are in the life of your church. Complete the rating scale and questions on your own before discussing your answers with the members of your small group.

Using the following scale, rate your level of involvement in the life of your church.

	Inactive				Somewhat Supportive			Active & Serving		
1. Financial giving	1	2	3	4	5	6	7	8	9	10
2. Attend at least 3 Sundays a month	1	2	3	4	5	6	7	8	9	10
3. Adult Sunday school class	1	2	3	4	5	6	7	8	9	10
4. Small-group Bible study	1	2	3	4	5	6	7	8	9	10
5. Accountability group	1	2	3	4	5	6	7	8	9	10
6. Ministry team	1	2	3	4	5	6	7	8	9	10
7. Using my spiritual gift	1	2	3	4	5	6	7	8	9	10
8. Praying for church ministries	1	2	3	4	5	6	7	8	9	10
9. Praying for pastoral staff	1	2	3	4	5	6	7	8	9	10
10. Praying for church missionaries	1	2	3	4	5	6	7	8	9	10
11. Short-term ministry trip	1	2	3	4	5	6	7	8	9	10
12. Involved in church leadership	1	2	3	4	5	6	7	8	9	10

Which one area of involvement did you rate the lowest?

Why did you give it the rating you did?

What would it take to move it up a notch or two?

How willing are you to work on that area? Why? What are some steps you could take in the next week?

SESSION 6
DISCOVERING YOUR SPIRITUAL GIFT

This session's activity will help you discover your spiritual gift so that you can find a place of fulfilling ministry. Follow the instructions in taking the survey. After you have completed it, get feedback from a close friend on the accuracy of your assessment. Then discuss your results with the men in your small group.

Sometimes we're reluctant to get involved in ministry because we're not sure what our spiritual gifts are. To begin thinking about it, complete the following self-evaluation (adapted from *Network Participant's Guide,* by Bruce Bugbee, Don Cousins, Bill Hybels). Read each of the descriptions below, and mark each according to how well you think it describes you.

Y = Yes, sounds just like me.

S = Somewhat or slightly like me.

N= No, that's not me at all.

? = I'm not sure.

In my opinion, I have strengths in . . . (circle your response)

1. Developing strategies or plans to reach identified goals; organizing people, tasks, and events; helping organizations or groups become more efficient; creating order out of organizational chaos.

        Y   S   N   ?   (Administration)

2. Pioneering new undertakings (such as a new church or ministry); serving in another country or community; adapting to different cultures and surroundings; being culturally aware and sensitive.

        Y   S   N   ?   (Apostleship)

3. Working creatively with wood, cloth, metal, paints, glass, and so on; working with different kinds of tools; making things with practical uses; designing or building things; working with my hands.

        Y   S   N   ?   (Craftsmanship)

4. Communicating with variety and creativity; developing and using particular artistic skills (arts, drama, music, photography, etc.); finding new and fresh ways to communicate ideas to others.

Y   S   N   ?   (Creative Communication)

5. Distinguishing between truth and error, good and evil; accurately judging character; seeing through phoniness or deceit; helping others to see rightness or wrongness in life situations.

Y   S   N   ?   (Discernment)

6. Strengthening and reassuring troubled people; encouraging or challenging people; motivating others to grow; supporting people who need to take action.

Y   S   N   ?   (Encouragement)

7. Looking for opportunities to build relationships with nonbelievers; communicating openly and effectively about my faith; talking about spiritual matters with nonbelievers.

Y   S   N   ?   (Evangelism)

8. Trusting God to answer prayer and encouraging others to do so; having confidence in God's continuing presence and ability to help even in difficult times; moving forward in spite of opposition.

Y   S   N   ?   (Faith)

9. Giving liberally and joyfully to people in financial need or projects requiring support; managing my money well in order to free more of it for giving.

Y   S   N   ?   (Giving)

10. Working behind the scenes to support the work of others; finding small things that need to be done and doing them without being asked; helping wherever needed, even with routine or mundane tasks.

Y   S   N   ?   (Helps)

11. Meeting new people and helping them to feel welcome; entertaining guests; opening my home to others who need a safe, supportive environment; setting people at ease in unfamiliar surroundings.

Y   S   N   ?   (Hospitality)

12. Continually offering to pray for others; expressing amazing trust in God's ability to provide; evidencing confidence in the Lord's protection; spending a lot of time praying.

Y   S   N   ?   (Intercession)

13. Carefully studying and researching subjects I want to understand better; sharing my knowledge and insights with others when asked; sometimes gaining information that is not attained by natural observation or means.

Y   S   N   ?   (Knowledge)

14. Taking responsibility for directing groups; motivating and guiding others to reach important goals; managing people and resources well; influencing others to perform to the best of their abilities.

Y   S   N   ?   (Leadership)

15. Empathizing with hurting people; patiently and compassionately supporting people through painful experiences; helping those generally regarded as undeserving or beyond help.

Y   S   N   ?   (Mercy)

16. Speaking with conviction in order to bring change in the lives of others; exposing cultural trends, teachings, or events that are morally wrong or harmful; boldly speaking truth even in places where it may be unpopular.

Y   S   N   ?   (Prophecy)

17. Faithfully providing long-term support and nurture for a group of people; providing guidance for the whole person; patiently but firmly nurturing others in their development as believers.

Y   S   N   ?   (Shepherding)

18. Studying, understanding, and communicating biblical truth; developing appropriate teaching material and presenting it effectively; communicating in ways that motivate others to change.

        Y   S   N   ?   (Teaching)

19. Seeing simple, practical solutions in the midst of conflict or confusion; giving helpful advice to others facing complicated life situations; helping people take practical action to solve real problems.

        Y   S   N   ?   (Wisdom)

Now that you have a better handle on your spiritual gift(s), where can you find opportunities to use it (them) in your church? In your small group? In other contexts?

✝ SESSION 7
WORSHIP AND REFLECTION

You've now spent six weeks going deeper into promise five. In this final session, spend the majority of your small-group time in prayer and worship to God. Thank Him for what He has accomplished in and through you so far, and ask for His help in continuing to grow and overcome any barriers that arise.

Finally, discuss with your group any changes you may need to make—based on your work over the last six sessions—in your plan for living out this promise. Record those changes, if any, below. Then transfer them to your daily planner/organizer.

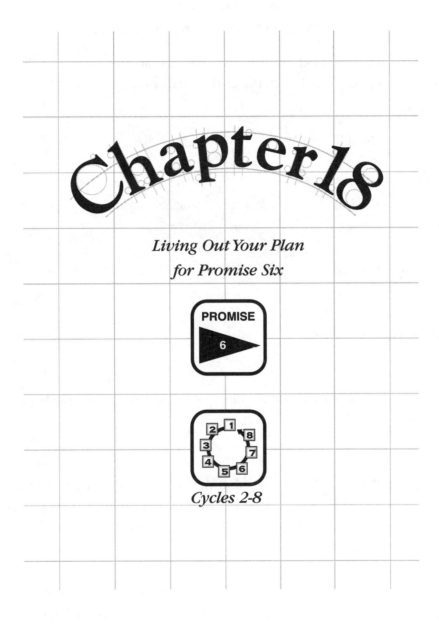

Chapter 18

*Living Out Your Plan
for Promise Six*

PROMISE
▶
6

Cycles 2-8

SESSION 1
UNITY, THE FINAL APOLOGETIC

In this session, you'll explore the scriptural foundation for unity. Read the passages as a group and discuss the questions that follow.

Read John 13:34-35; 17:20-21

What was Christ's desire for His church?

Why do you think He was so concerned about that issue?

What forces fight against unity?

Who was Christ praying for?

Is unity something just for a local church, or is it to characterize the larger Body of Christ as well? Why?

The late Dr. Francis Schaeffer said that the unity of the church was the final apologetic—the convincing evidence—that Jesus Christ was sent by God. In your opinion, how is unity a convincing proof of Jesus' deity?

In light of what you've learned, how committed are you, individually and as a group, to promoting unity within the church? How can you do that?

SESSION 2
THE PERILS OF PREJUDICE

This session focuses on the dangers of favoritism. Read the following passage, and discuss the questions during your small-group meeting.

Read James 2:1-12.

What type of prejudice was James warning against?

What other types of prejudice are there? Think of as many as you can.

What are the effects of prejudice?

Think of a time when someone prejudged you. Explain the situation. How did you feel?

How can you start to overcome the tendency to prejudge people based on external characteristics like level of prosperity or skin color?

SESSION 3
EXAMINING YOUR PREJUDICES

In this session, you'll come face to face with some of your own prejudices. Do the following self-evaluation on your own before discussing your answers with your small group.

How would you respond in the following circumstances? Circle the answer that best describes how you honestly feel.

	Shun/refuse			Welcome with open arms	
1. A person of another color invites me to lunch.	1	2	3	4	5
2. A co-worker who is generally considered unattractive asks me for help.	1	2	3	4	5
3. A church in my denomination invites our church to participate in an outreach project.	1	2	3	4	5
4. A church in a *different* denomination invites us to participate in an outreach project.	1	2	3	4	5
5. A person who speaks a foreign language moves in next door.	1	2	3	4	5
6. A young man of another color invites my daughter out on a date.	1	2	3	4	5
7. My son wants to date a young woman who is blind.	1	2	3	4	5
8. A person of another color invites me to a Bible study.	1	2	3	4	5
9. A person of a different economic status invites me to a Bible study.	1	2	3	4	5

10. A church in a poorer section of town
suggests we form a sister church relationship. 1   2   3   4   5

11. A person of another color is appointed
as my new boss.   1   2   3   4   5

12. A woman is appointed as my new boss.   1   2   3   4   5

13. A Christian of a different denomination
is appointed as my new boss.   1   2   3   4   5

14. My favorite restaurant changes ownership and
is now operated by a person of another color.   1   2   3   4   5

15. My turn comes at the post office, and the
clerk is a handicapped person.   1   2   3   4   5

16. The gas station nearest my home or office
is run by an obviously uneducated person.   1   2   3   4   5

17. I signed up for a men's accountability
group, only to discover that another member
is a person of a different color.   1   2   3   4   5

18. As I head for the checkout at the grocery
store, I can choose between a clerk of my
color or one of another color. The person
of another color has the shortest line.   1   2   3   4   5

19. I call my dentist to schedule an appointment
because I have a broken tooth. However,
I discover that he is out of town and his
substitute is a person from another country.   1   2   3   4   5

20. My college-age daughter wants to bring a
person from a disadvantaged family home
for Thanksgiving dinner.   1   2   3   4   5

A Short Course in Overcoming Prejudice

Perhaps this self-test has revealed some prejudice on the part of your small-group members. As a group, read and discuss the three suggestions below as a start to honoring God by learning to love all His people.

1. ACKNOWLEDGE THAT CHRIST IS NO RESPECTER OF PERSONS.

In Christ, there is no Jew or Greek, slave or freeman, male or female (see Galatians 3:26-28). Kneeling at the foot of the cross, everyone is equal. Read John 19 about the crucifixion of Christ. Then picture Him dying for those you circled as having problems with.

2. UNDERSTAND THAT PREJUDICE IS A LEARNED BEHAVIOR.

If you struggle with accepting those of different colors or denominations, ask yourself if it's largely a historical issue—that is, thoughts or complaints passed down from others to whom you're still being loyal, even if they're totally wrong. Start praying now that walls would come down if you come from a line of hate or bitter division.

3. LET A PERSON BREAK A STEREOTYPE.

It's easier to label someone if we haven't spoken with him. Pray that the Lord would link your church and family with other believers who are different from yourself. Pray also for opportunities to build a bridge to someone God puts in your life, whether it be a neighbor, a co-worker, a foreign student in your community, or a parent of one of your children's classmates.

Pray that God would help you to see with His eyes and love with His heart those who are different from you.

🦾 SESSION 4
VALUING THE PARTS OF THE BODY, PART 1

The focus of this session is the value of other parts of the Body of Christ. Read the passage, and discuss the questions in your small group.

Read 1 Corinthians 12:12-27.

What is Paul's point in this passage?

Have you ever been guilty of what Paul is talking about? Explain the situation.

Are there parts of the Body of Christ that you consider to be of less value than others? What has led you to that evaluation?

After reading Paul's instructions in 1 Corinthians 12, how do you reconcile your opinion? What should you do about it?

What other members of the Body of Christ do you need to ask forgiveness from because you have devalued them? When and how, in the course of the next couple of weeks, will you do that?

SESSION 5
VALUING THE PARTS OF THE BODY, PART 2

In the last session, you saw the importance Scripture gives to all parts of the Body of Christ, the church. Now discover the value of those various parts from firsthand observation. Schedule a time to complete this activity, and then talk about what you learned.

As a small group, visit a worship service in a church of either another color or a different denomination from your own.

What was similar to your church?

What was different from your church?

How did the people express their relationship with Jesus Christ?

What did you learn about diversity within the Body?

SESSION 6
LIVING OUT BIBLICAL UNITY

Below is a case study about a church struggling against the forces of prejudice and disunity. Read the study, and then discuss the questions that follow during your small-group session.

Marc was chairman of the council of elders at First Church. On the elders' meeting agenda one night was the thorny issue of community outreach. Tension had been building for several months and could no longer be avoided. First Church was 75 years old. When it began, it was in the center of a white, upper-middle-class neighborhood. But over the years, the neighborhood had changed both racially and economically. The population was now predominantly Hispanic, with significant Asian and African-American communities mixed in. Whites were a small minority. The church, however, still reflected its roots; the majority of the congregation was white, though the people had long since moved out of the area.

Six months ago, the youth pastor began an outreach to the neighborhood junior high students. Many responded to the Monday gym nights and Friday night concerts, and several attended the Thursday evening Bible studies. Then came the summer backpacking trip that escalated the tension to a fever pitch. It seemed the neighborhood kids registered and filled two-thirds of the spaces on the bus before the church kids had the chance to sign up.

Several parents who were regular attenders and faithful financial givers objected to the neighborhood students' being with their children. "The neighborhood kids are vandals," they said. "They're a bad influence. We don't want them corrupting our children." The parents argued that there should be two separate youth programs, one for church kids and one for neighborhood kids. "If that isn't approved," they asserted, "we're leaving the church."

In his devotions the morning of the meeting, Marc meditated on Romans 14:19: "Let us therefore make every effort to do what leads to peace and to mutual edification."

What advice would you give Marc? What should he say to the other elders? To the concerned parents? To the youth pastor? To the neighborhood kids?

How can Marc encourage the church to pursue peace and mutual edification?

What issues threaten the unity of the believers in your own church? How can you be a peacemaker in that situation?

✝ SESSION 7
WORSHIP AND REFLECTION

You've now spent six weeks going deeper into promise six. In this final session, spend the majority of your small-group time in prayer and worship to God. Thank Him for what He has accomplished in and through you so far, and ask for His help in continuing to grow and overcome any barriers that arise.

Finally, discuss with your group any changes you may need to make—based on your work over the last six sessions—in your plan for living out this promise. Record those changes, if any, below. Then transfer them to your daily planner/organizer.

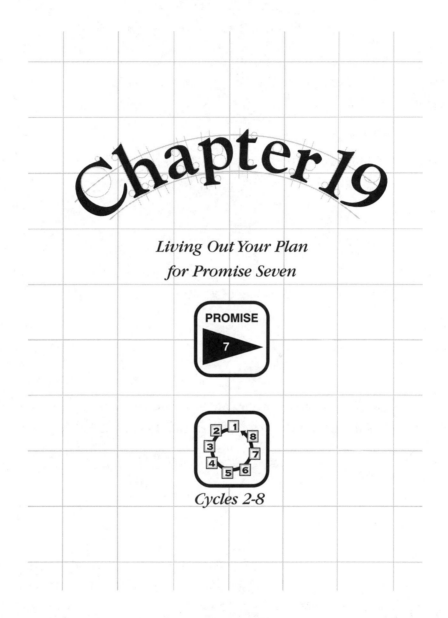

Chapter 19

Living Out Your Plan
for Promise Seven

PROMISE
7

Cycles 2-8

SESSION 1
THE POWER OF FRIENDSHIP

This session, focus on banding together to introduce someone to Jesus Christ. During your small-group session, read the passage, discuss the questions, and begin a prayer list.

Read Mark 2:1-12.

What was the person's need?

What effect did his friends' faith have on Jesus' forgiving the man's sins and healing him? (Hint: Notice the beginning of verse 5.)

Sometimes we don't witness for Christ with an individual because we consider the person beyond hope. Who do you know that it would take four guys carrying the person to bring him to salvation?

Start a list of individuals for whom you and your small group can pray. (Use the spaces below.) Ask God to give you the opportunity to "carry them to Jesus." End your group session by praying for these people.

_____   _____

_____   _____

_____   _____

SESSION 2
THE WITNESS OF A CHANGED LIFE

This session's assignment will help prepare you to tell another person what Jesus Christ means to you. Work on the assignment by yourself, and then practice it in your small group.

Read 1 Peter 3:15. One of the answers you can give is to tell how your life has changed since you became a Christian.

Using the following guidelines, write out your testimony. Practice giving it to the members of your small group. Then pick one person you can tell it to this week.

• Tell what your life was like before you became a Christian. (Think in terms of your feelings, goals, priorities, language, the health of your relationships, etc.)

• Explain how you became a Christian.
   What factors led you to recognize your need for forgiveness?

   Who introduced you to Christ?

• Describe how your life is different now that you're a Christian.

Write out the name of the person to whom you want to tell your story:

_____

SESSION 3
THE WITNESS OF A GREAT CHURCH

A great church can be another powerful witness of God's love and grace. In this session, you'll discover what makes a great church and discuss how your church can become one. Read each passage of Scripture, and talk about how your church can put its principles into practice.

Rick Warren has said, "A great commitment (Matthew 10:37-38) to the Great Commandment (Matthew 22:37-39) and the Great Commission (Matthew 28:19-20) makes a great church (Matthew 16:18-19)."

Do you agree with that assessment? Why or why not?

In what ways does your church best meet that definition of greatness?

In which areas could your church use some extra effort?

Applying that definition to *yourself*, how great is your life?

In which areas could you use some extra effort?

SESSION 4
THE SECOND CHANCE

The Bible tells an instructive story of a man who received a second chance to tell others about their need to get right with God. Read the passage before coming to the small-group meeting so you're prepared to discuss the questions.

Read the book of Jonah. (Its four short chapters will take only 10-15 minutes.)

What did God instruct Jonah to do?

Why do you think he resisted God's desire? Could it be that he was prejudiced? Might he have thought the Ninevites beyond hope—that God could never save them?

Think of a time when you or someone else had the opportunity to present the gospel and didn't do it. Explain the situation and what happened.

One of the most comforting verses in all of Scripture is Jonah 3:1. Reread it. Remind yourself that even though you might have failed to speak up for Christ in the past, God can and will give you another opportunity.

Pick one of the people you listed during session 1, and ask God to give you the chance to speak to him or her this week. As a group, discuss the possibility of hosting a social event to which each member could invite someone on his list and where the gospel would be presented by one or more men from the group.

SESSION 5
THE GREAT COMMISSION

During this session, allow God to place on your heart another country and people that need the gospel. Read the verses listed, and discuss the questions that follow. Close your time by praying for the country and missionary you selected.

Read Matthew 28:19-20 and Acts 1:8.

Where were the disciples to take the gospel?

If you were to apply Christ's command to your own life, where would your Jerusalem be? Your Judea and Samaria? What would you consider to be the ends of the earth?

As a group, decide on an "ends of the earth" country that you can adopt and pray for. Do some research. (Pick up a copy of *Operation World,* by Patrick Johnstone.)
• What kind of people live there?

• What is the predominant religion?

• What are the major needs?

• What needs do they have that you might be able to meet yourselves?

• What missionary ministers in that country? (Ask your pastor for suggestions.) What needs does he or she have?

• How can you pray for the person?

• Consider contacting the person and becoming a prayer supporter.

SESSION 6
SACRIFICE AND SERVICE

In this session, think about what it might cost you to serve God. During your small-group time, read the quotation below and discuss the questions that follow.

"He is no fool who gives up what he cannot keep to gain what he cannot lose" (Jim Eliot).

During session 3, you learned that witnessing for Christ is one of the hallmarks of a great church. In session 5, you began to pray for people in another country who need to learn about Jesus. What if God decided that *you* were the answer to your own prayer and He sent you to tell them about Himself?

How would you feel if God wanted you to go to another country to present the gospel? Why?

What would you need to give up to be obedient and follow God?

List as many reasons as you can for why it would be too difficult for you to go.

List as many reasons as you can for why it would be easy for you to go.

Pray that God would help each of you in your group to be willing to follow Him wherever He leads and at whatever cost.

✝ SESSION 7
WORSHIP AND REFLECTION

You've now spent six weeks going deeper into promise seven. In this final session, spend the majority of your small-group time in prayer and worship to God. Thank Him for what He has accomplished in and through you so far, and ask for His help in continuing to grow and overcome any barriers that arise.

Finally, discuss with your group any changes you may need to make—based on your work over the last six sessions—in your plan for living out this promise. Record those changes, if any, below. Then transfer them to your daily planner/organizer.

Part IV

The Making of a

GODLY MAN

FINAL THOUGHTS AND
ADDITIONAL RESOURCES

Chapter 20

WORKING

AND RESTING

IN HIM

Writer Brennan Manning tells the story of a man named Marty who had come to know Christ late in life. Now Marty lay dying, and Manning was asked if he would visit the old man and pray for him.

When he arrived, he found Marty sitting up in his bed, with an empty chair pulled close to him. "Oh," Manning said, "I didn't know you were expecting company."

"I'm not," Marty said, beckoning him to come and sit down.

They had a nice visit, Manning prayed for Marty, and finally Manning got up to leave the room.

"Could you please shut the door for a minute before you leave?" Marty asked him.

With the door shut, Marty breathed heavily and said, "Let me tell you about why that chair's beside my bed. You see, I didn't become a Christian until just a few years ago, and I found it really difficult to pray. That's when a friend told me, 'Marty, just pull up a chair, and picture that you're talking to Jesus face to face. That's all prayer is.'

"Pastor," Marty said, "that's why the chair's there. It helps me when I want to pray. But I don't want the nurses to see me talking to a chair. They'll think I'm a little off. Know what I mean?"

Manning assured him there was nothing wrong with his physical reminder that he could come face to face with Jesus in prayer, and then he said good-bye.

A few days later, the phone rang. It was Marty's daughter, calling to say her father had passed away. "It meant a lot to me that you'd take the time to go and pray for him," she said.

He assured her it was an honor, and then she said, "But one thing is still bothering me. When he died, he wasn't in his bed. The nurse found him sitting on the floor next to his bed . . . *with his head lying on a chair.*"

All of us who have had a part in putting this workbook together pray that at the end of your time with it, you'll have seen Jesus in a clearer, more compelling, more comforting way than ever before. We also pray that others in your family and world will see the difference God's Word and love have made in your life.

FIRST DOWN, LIFETIME TO GO

In the book of Hebrews, the writer set a goal for every Christian and an unusual way to reach it. He wrote, "There remains, then, a Sabbath-rest for the people of God; for anyone who enters God's rest also rests from his own work, just as God did from his" (4:9-10).

In our strained-out, burned-out, stressed-out world, rest is something most of us would love to appropriate! But listen to how that rest is achieved.

"Let us, therefore, make every effort to enter that rest" (4:11).

Doesn't that sound contradictory? *Work hard to enter into rest?*

Perhaps by now, however, you've already seen the truth to this biblical paradox. Namely, there's a rest that comes from committing our lives to doing what's right.

In creation, God's effort in speaking forth the universe was followed by a "Sabbath-rest." So, too, we're to be diligent in living for Christ, with the result that we go to sleep more at peace with ourselves and more rested emotionally and spiritually as we've done His will and work that day. And at our final rest, we'll hear God's comforting words, "Well done, good and faithful servant."

You've now spent weeks and months in discussion, prayer, worship, and instruction with your small group. That's a lot of work! Yet you've also been challenged to take time out at the end of each set of exercises in part 3 to "rest" and worship the Lord Jesus. And this process of living out God's Word and then "resting" and worshiping Him isn't just part of a curriculum. It's a lifestyle choice.

With that in mind, here's one last tool we'd encourage you to fill out. It's something we recommend you do on a semiannual basis to help maintain the good work you've done, and to go even further. The evening or afternoon you spend with your spouse or small group revising, reflecting, and maintaining your spiritual growth plan will keep you pointed toward His best and thankful for how far He's brought you.

REACHING YOUR "HORIZON POINT". . . AND BEYOND

Here's the thinking behind this last tool: By going through this workbook, and after completing the reinforcing "cycles" for each promise, you've spent almost a year on your plan! That's profitable time spent developing spiritual muscle and daily growth "habits" that affect actions and attitudes. It's important not to just set your plan aside now, but instead to continue to refer to it as you work toward your spiritual goals.

Take your Promise Keepers planner/organizer (or whatever calendar you use), and write down "Review my spiritual growth plan" six months from today, and again six months from that date.

Remember, you'll tend to get out of this spiritual growth plan whatever you "inspect," not just what you "expect." And setting a semiannual time to see how you're progressing toward Christlikeness is some of the best "planning" time you'll ever spend.

The form we've created to help with this is designed to capture new things you've learned and needed changes God may have impressed on you. It also encourages you to keep a prayer and praise journal and to submit your plan to a regular "reality check."

This reality check is actually a simple evaluation you conduct with one person inside your home (preferably your spouse if you're married) and one person who sees you in the workplace or has other regular contact with you. Ask them to evaluate the areas you've grown in, as well as issues, attitudes, or goals they'd encourage you to work on. These suggestions and evaluations can then be worked into your plan as the Lord leads. *Feel free to make multiple copies of this form for future semiannual evaluations.*

SIX MONTH REVIEW & RECOMMITMENT SHEET

DATE _____

PROMISE 1:

Changes to my plan:_____

_____

_____

_____

Further insights:_____

_____

_____

PROMISE 2:

Changes to my plan:_____

_____

_____

_____

Further insights:_____

_____

_____

PROMISE 3:

Changes to my plan:_____

_____

_____

_____

Further insights:_____

_____

_____

PROMISE 4:

Changes to my plan:_____

_____

_____

Further insights:_____

_____

_____

PROMISE 5:

Changes to my plan:_____

_____

_____

_____

Further insights:_____

_____

_____

PROMISE 6:

Changes to my plan:_____

_____

_____

_____

Further insights:_____

_____

_____

PROMISE 7:

Changes to my plan:_____

_____

_____

_____

Further insights:_____

_____

_____

SIX MONTH PRAYER/PRAISE JOURNAL

DATE _____

Answered prayers for myself or someone else:

_____
_____
_____
_____
_____
_____
_____
_____

REALITY CHECK: I've interviewed two people who know me well and asked them for honest feedback on these two questions:

"How have I grown during this period of time?" and "What areas do I still need to work on?"

[ ] Areas of growth:

_____
_____
_____
_____

[ ] Areas I still need work on:

_____
_____
_____
_____

Traveling without a clear destination becomes tedious and pointless. Keep pointing your life toward the Savior, however, and you'll never lack for purpose, direction, or motivation. And be sure to put your new/revised action points in your daily planner/organizer.

BE STRONG AND COURAGEOUS

On December 14, 1862, something happened that for one brief moment stopped an entire battle.

Fully a dozen times, Union soldiers charged across an open field, trying to take a hill called Marye's Heights at Fredericksburg, Virginia. Their valor wasn't enough.

In 12 attempts, not one Union soldier made it to the stone wall at the far end of the field. That wall was heavily defended by Confederate troops who poured devastating rifle and canister shot across the field. Colonel Joshua Chamberlain of Maine was to recount, "My ears were filled with the cries and groans of the wounded. The ghastly faces of the dead almost made a wall around me."

With each assault, the wounded piled up. They lay suffering in the December cold, slowly freezing to death on the open plain, wracked by pain and thirst caused by their wounds.

But then something happened that astonished men on both sides of the battle.

During a lull in the fighting, Sergeant Richard Rowland Kirkland of the Second South Carolina regiment, Confederate States Army, felt he had to do something in the name of Christ for those men. He loaded himself with borrowed canteens, then leaped over the wall and walked to the nearest Union sufferer. Kirkland knelt and gave him water, made him more comfortable, and then moved on to the next . . . and the next . . . and the next.

For an hour and a half, not one shot was fired from either side.

All because one man stepped out.

Men to whom Kirkland reached out still died that day, but not a man left that field who didn't remember "The Angel of Marye's Heights."

Our prayer for you is that the Holy Spirit would prompt, encourage, and sustain you so that even in the midst of life's battles, you'll be more concerned with living for Christ than with your own life. May the Lord help you to live out the charge He gave to another brave warrior named Joshua:

Be strong and courageous. Do not be terrified; do not be discouraged,
for the LORD your God will be with you wherever you go.
(Joshua 1:9)

ADDITIONAL RESOURCES

Go the Distance
(Colorado Springs, Colo.: Focus on the Family, 1996)
Live a life of no regrets and cross life's finish line confident you've run a good race! Like a how-to manual for claiming the prize, this book is packed with training tips for building your faith's endurance. Alongside such inspirational coaches as John Trent, Jack Hayford, Chuck Colson, and others, you'll learn to pace yourself through the years and reap the reward of faithful promise keeping! Also available on audiocassette.

The Power of a Promise Kept
(Colorado Springs, Colo.: Focus on the Family, 1995)
Take an up-close and personal look at men who made a commitment at a Promise Keepers event and are now testifying to the incredible difference putting faith into action has made in their lives. Also available on audiocassette.

Seven Promises of a Promise Keeper
(Colorado Springs, Colo.: Focus on the Family, 1994)
In this best-seller, leading authors like Bill Bright, Dr. James Dobson, Jack Hayford, Howard Hendricks, and Gary Smalley reveal how it's possible to cultivate life-changing relationships with your wife, children, friends, church, and Lord. Also available on audiocassette.

Applying the Seven Promises (Promise Builders Bible study series)
Bob Horner, Ron Ralston, David Sunde (Colorado Springs, Colo.: Focus on the Family, 1996)
This easy-to-use Bible study integrates God's Word into every aspect of life.

The Promise Keeper at Work (Promise Builders Bible study series)
Bob Horner, Ron Ralston, David Sunde (Colorado Springs, Colo.: Focus on the Family, 1996)
This second study in the series shows how to bring faith and integrity into the workplace.

The PK Planner/Organizer
As we give our hearts to God, He will give direction for our everyday lives. Promise Keepers presents a planner/organizer to help a man stay on track with the direction God has provided. This planner will assist you in focusing on your daily relationships with Christ, your family, your brothers, and others as you allow God's Spirit to establish the discipline in your life needed to keep your promises.

These books can be found at your local Christian bookstore. For more information about these and other resources, contact Promise Keepers at 800-456-7594.